Write for Children

Writing for children is not about writing little stories, it is about writing big stories shorter. Children's literature is an art form in its own right, and this book is for anyone who wants not just to write for children, but to write *well* for them. It looks at four main areas of the writing process:

- **Crafting and the Critically Creative:** a critical look at children's literature and the craft of writing.
- **Write the Rights/Know the Wrongs:** fundamental storytelling techniques such as storyline, characters and viewpoint.
- **Write the Height:** writing for different age groups, including sensory books, picture books, short fiction, teen and series fiction.
- **Write the Rest:** a guide to other areas of children's literature including biography, humour, poetry, film, new media and non-fiction.

This comprehensive and accessible book goes beyond the standard 'how to' format to help writers learn the finely balanced craft of writing for children. It will be an indispensable handbook for aspiring and practising children's authors.

Andrew Melrose is a principal lecturer at King Alfred's University College, Winchester, where he is Director of the MA in Writing for Children. He has written over 40 children's books and films.

Golden age for kid lit

After the disgraceful and somewhat dated, 'what is literature' debate that followed the Whitbread prize's Harry Potter versus Beowulf debacle, how refreshing it is to see that four out of the nation's top five favourite authors write for children (Dahl beats all competitors, March 10). Isn't it time we finally consigned the kid lit, poor cousin, low culture, slings and arrows, literary contempt back to the dark ages, from whence it came? A visit to any bookstore will confirm there has never been a better time for children's literature. We are living in the golden age. Let's at least take it seriously.

Dr Andrew Melrose
Brighton March 2000
Cartoon by Merrily Harpur
Guardian

Write for Children

Andrew Melrose

RoutledgeFalmer
Taylor & Francis Group

LONDON AND NEW YORK

First published 2002
by RoutledgeFalmer
11 New Fetter Lane, London EC4P 4EE

Simultaneously published in the USA and Canada
by RoutledgeFalmer
29 West 35th Street, New York, NY 10001

Reprinted 2004

RoutledgeFalmer is an imprint of the Taylor & Francis Group

© 2002 Andrew Melrose

Typeset in Goudy by
Keystroke, Jacaranda Lodge, Wolverhampton
Printed and bound in Great Britain by
TJ International Ltd, Padstow, Cornwall

British Library Cataloguing in Publication Data
A catalogue record for this book is available from the British Library

Library of Congress Cataloging in Publication Data
A catalog record for this book has been requested

Melrose, Andrew, 1954–
     Write for children / Andrew Melrose.
          p. cm.
     Includes bibliographical references (p.) and index.
     ISBN 0–415–25158–3 (pbk.)
     1. Children's literature–Authorship. I. Title.

PN147.5 .M45 2001
808′.06′8–dc21   2001052012

ISBN 0–415–25158–3

Contents

Introduction   ix

1   **Crafting and the critically creative**   1

2   **Write the rights/know the wrongs**   15

Story   15
Characters   22
Viewpoint   29
Pyramid plot structure   42
Dialogue   63
Prose   74

3   **Write the height**   83

Understanding age groups   83
Sensory books   86
Picture books   90
Fiction   109
Submission   138

4   Write the rest   140

Non-fiction   140
Poetry (an introduction)   152
Film and new media (an introduction)   155

Notes   157
Bibliography   159
Index   164

For Abbi and Daniel who like to read good writing

And shall we just carelessly allow children to hear any casual tales which may be devised by casual persons, and to receive into their minds ideas for the most part the very opposite of those which we should wish them to have when they are grown up?
We cannot!

Plato, The Republic

Introduction

Writers for children have long been heralded as the poor relations in the literary family and it has to be said that there is a long historical reasoning behind this. But things are changing, and have been for some time now. Children's literature as an art form in its own right is starting to receive the recognition it richly deserves. This book is designed for anyone who has ever considered writing for children and cares enough to want to write well for them.

The learning is worth it. The reading life of a child is a short one, around ten years all in all before they are expected to grapple with Shakespeare, Dickens and the various examination-led authors who take them out of childhood into the dark forest of the grown-ups. How well is your writing leading children down the path of experience before they hit the trees? Are they entering the forest unprepared, inexperienced and bewildered or has your writing given them the confidence to go boldly? When writing for children these are the questions you must ask yourself. These are the questions this book addresses.

Then some more questions are addressed. Do you write *at* or *for* children? Are you giving children what you think they want without knowing what they need? Is your writing good enough for them to read? Each question has to be considered carefully.

The first issue the book addresses is 'Crafting and the critically creative'. Here I look objectively at writing for children and the craft issues involved in an effort to get you to take your creative task seriously. Try not to skip this first section because it crucially sets up the premise of the book by asking you to raise your critical awareness. Writing is not just about sitting down and writing one word after another. It is about the craft of writing, and you need to know why this is important.

I then go on to address what I have called 'Write the rights/know the wrongs'. The issues raised here become obvious because the craft of writing is addressed in more detail. By looking at story, characters, viewpoint, the pyramid plot structure, dialogue and prose, I highlight the most fundamental storytelling techniques, giving examples where appropriate, to help you to identify your own strengths and weaknesses. There is much necessary overlapping in these sections because they interact with each other but they will help you to understand the craft you are trying to master.

In 'Write the height' I address specifics in the area of writing for children. Age and experience are huge factors in writing for children, thus sections entitled 'Understanding age groups', 'Sensory books', 'Picture books', 'Short fiction', 'Longer fiction', 'Teen fiction' and 'Series fiction' are designed to assist you in developing your ideas and knowing for whom you are writing. This is crucial in writing for children because your audience is a variable one, governed by experience and cognitive ability. This chapter concludes with a section on submitting to publishers.

The final chapter of the book, 'Write the rest', addresses non-fiction, biography, humour, poetry, film and new media. Thus it is hoped that the book will serve as a guide to writing for children in all its myriad forms. My aim is to introduce you to the thrills and spills, footholds and faultlines in the craft of writing for children. Each section has critical commentary as well as hints and exercises.

It is important to remember that this is not a 'how to write' book. It is a handbook for the craft of writing for children which explains how to improve what you have already written. The book works on the same premise that you wouldn't try to play a Mozart piano concerto, paint the *Mona Lisa* or produce a new stained-glass window for Winchester Cathedral without lessons in the craft. As I write, there are some 10,000 books for children being produced in the UK alone each year. In terms of quality, sometimes I wonder why the authors bothered. I urge you to try to address this. Don't just write for children. Write well for them. Give them the literary experience they deserve; it behoves us to give them the best.

There are a number of people I wish to thank. My Writing for Children Master's Degree students, past and present, at King Alfred's, University College Winchester, have been kind enough to point out the rights and wrongs, the highs and lows and the successes and failures in teaching such material. Their conversations and contributions to tutorials have been invaluable. Anna Powell provided the illustrations, Diana Kimpton allowed me to reproduce material and her website, www.wordpool.co.uk, is well worth a visit. But most of all I thank my family for giving me the time and space needed to write and research. Without them it would have been a poorer book. Of course, all errors and failings are acknowledged as mine alone.

Andrew Melrose
Winchester, June 2001

1 Crafting and the critically creative

Usually the easiest way into any book is to start at the beginning, but when you are writing for children you have to know where the beginning is – and it is not always where you think. Let me make a start, then, by advising you of the very first thing you need to think about before you begin writing for children. It is very simple and straight-forward: If you think writing for children is just practice for writing for grown-ups, think again. Remember this: it is important!

Writing for any audience is about respecting that audience.

Writing for a child can't begin from the premise that it demands less skill than writing for an adult because the truth is that it simply doesn't. Nor should it be used simply as practice while your adult magnum opus is germinating.

All readers, children included, should have the quality of writing they deserve. It is entirely appropriate that we give them the best we have. Added to which, writers cannot assume they are giving children what they want without knowing what they need. This is crucial.

The splendid Italian writer Italo Calvino (1986: 85) once wrote: 'Literature is not school. Literature must presuppose a public that is more cultured, and *more cultured than the writer himself.* Whether or not such a public exists is unimportant.' I fully endorse this and it applies to children too. Don't be fooled into thinking children are second-rate repositories for second-rate stories. Children *need* the best and it behoves you to give them it. Children are also very astute judges. They are just as critical of books as are their adult counterparts. They can spot a fraud a mile away. But ask yourself this: why would anyone want to give them less than their best, and perhaps just as crucially, do they know what that is? And to this we might add, is *your* best good enough and do you know what your best is? This book is designed to help you tease this out.

That's not to say you can't write for both adults and children. Anne Fine and Penelope Lively manage this very well, as do many others, but they do so with respect for *all* of their audiences. One is not subordinate to the other.

However,

writing for children requires more skill than writing for adults.

Master the craft of writing for children and you will be able to write for anyone. This may seem a little contentious, and I know many, perhaps those working at the cutting edge of literature, might well disagree (although I suspect Salman Rushdie is very proud of *Haroun and the Sea of Stories*). But I truly believe there is much more to this statement than just a pithy slogan. It is something that gets to the very core of writing. Throughout this book we will be considering the precision required when writing for children. If you pay attention to all of the issues I raise in this book and apply them to all your writing with vigilance, you will at least be setting yourself a good precedent. But this book is only an aid to help you write better, to help you to craft the critically creative. No one can write for you.

Everyone who can write can be a writer, but the secret to writing well is getting the right words in the right order.

I run a Masters programme in writing for children[1] and every year, in my introduction to new students, I tell them this secret. Imparting the secret isn't too hard. Indeed, it seems so perfectly obvious that you might think there is no point in reading on. But to expect anyone to get it right immediately would be a bit like asking me to play a Rachmaninov piano concerto after learning only the rudiments of that fine instrument (I could probably play all the notes, and even some extra ones, though not necessarily in the right order – and for those of you old enough to remember, the Morecambe and Wise gag with André Previn immediately springs to mind). The writing has to be crafted skilfully into an intelligible narrative.

Writing is a craft!

In the same way that one has to learn to play and practise the piano before reaching any stage of competency, a writer has to learn the rudiments and practise their craft.

The purpose of this book, then, is to address the very issue of craft. As Seamus Heaney (1979: 47) once wrote, 'Craft is the skill of making . . . Learning the craft is learning to turn the windlass at the well.' When T.S. Eliot dedicated *The Wasteland* to Ezra Pound, it was to *il miglior fabbro* – which can be loosely translated as 'the better craftsman'. Indeed the philosopher Walter Benjamin described the storyteller as the craftsman who stamps his own style on to the telling of the story. Even on the printed page the palimpsest trace of the craftsman comes through to reveal himself or herself.

Providing you have a story to tell (after all, what is the purpose of writing for anyone if not to tell a story?)[2] this book is about helping you to craft the right words in the right order, with the specific aim of being able to address children. Creative writing involves mastering the craft of writing, so that you learn the necessary skills to write *intentionally*.

Nevertheless, like all books, this one has to be more than a simple 'how to do it' if it is to be worth reading at all. It follows that if a book on myths is itself a kind of myth, as Claude Lévi-Strauss once said, likewise a book on craft is itself a craft. This book on the craft of writing for children is written in order to help us identify, observe and address the links between critic and author. It is to help us discern the difference between storytelling and telling stories; the difference between the authentic and inauthentic, where half a story can tell the bigger lie and a whole story is not necessarily wholesome. This means we also have to be able to address wider issues like understanding stereotypes, reading subtextual meaning, and becoming aware of the historical, aesthetic and cultural significance of what we write. Thus, each section will have a *critical perspective* based on research. And if you found this paragraph a little opaque, don't worry about that; everything will become clearer. Because while these issues are not easy, there is a simple way of telling them and you should not be fazed by highfalutin rhetoric that often masquerades as scholarship. There is no need to be afraid of erudition, but it should not come at the expense of clarity of thought and expression. This book is written for you and I will be addressing you directly.

To write well for children requires such a fine attention to detail that it's crucial to know for whom you are writing. I call it *writing the height*. Only adults write for children and this in itself is fraught with difficulties. Time and again I tell my students that when they are writing for children they have to try to gauge the height they are writing for, then aim to maintain it. If the average height of an eight-year-old child is a little more than a metre, then you have to write at that height. You have to try to see the world from that height.

But I don't mean physically. I mean write the height in terms of development and experience. You have to try to write the world from a POV (point of view) that an eight-year-old child will recognise. All the intellectualising in the world will not replace that basic need. But it is not easy. When trying to visualise the world from a metaphorically childlike, although not childish, view, you are presented with another problem. In her book on Peter Pan, Jacqueline Rose addressed this issue:

> Children's fiction is impossible, not in the sense that it cannot be written (that would be nonsense), but in that it hangs on an impossibility, one which rarely speaks. This is the impossible relation between adult and child . . . Children's fiction sets up a world in which the adult comes first (author, maker, giver) and the child comes after (reader, product, receiver), but where neither of them enter the space in between.
>
> (Rose 1994: 1–2)

This space is one of experience. The gap is between the child and the author or parent's experience, between the experience of authority and the child's inexperience. It is the writer's job to try to close the gap. How can this be achieved? Well, knowing about it helps, but there is more to it. Rightly, in my view, the children's psychoanalyst Adam Phillips observes that:

Children unavoidably treat their parents as though they were the experts on life . . . but children make demands on adults which adults don't know what to do with . . . once they [children] learn to talk they create, and suffer, a certain unease about what they can do with words. Paradoxically, it is the adult's own currency – words – that reveal to them the limit of adult authority . . . Adults can nurture children . . . but they do not have the answers . . . what they can do is tell children stories about the connections.

(Phillips 1995: 1–2)

This idea of *nurture* is a persuasive one which writers for children must be aware of. For example, an issue like age matters in terms of the reader's experience. A child who has not lived very long cannot have the same 'historical horizon' or the same developed sense of reflection and anticipation as someone older.

Nevertheless, just as height doesn't equate with experience and development, age and reading age are not necessarily the same. They are only benchmarks. An example I used recently still holds true:

a fourteen-year-old boy with the reading ability of, say, a nine-year-old [not all that uncommon] will not want a nine-year-old child's story, when what he is already interested in is football, computers and masturbation. Just as a thirteen-year-old girl who is interested in belly-button piercing is hardly going to be stimulated by a book targeted at nine- to thirteen-year-olds when she is already passionate about Jane Austen's *Pride and Prejudice*.

(Melrose 2001: 14)

If you have little contact with children yourself, speak to those who have regular contact, teachers and parents, for example, and they will tell you this is not a fiction or a worst-case scenario. The biggest problem with literacy is keeping the reader (even the good reader[3]) interested in reading. Thus, you have to write for them.

Writing the height, then, is about awareness of child development. It is about knowing for whom you are writing. That's not to say your story should be shackled into a constraining straitjacket. The story has to be able to breathe its own life, but you have to be aware of who your reader is. If I am repeating this it is because it needs to be stressed. There is no point in being the best tailor in the world if no one can wear the suit you have so carefully and exquisitely stitched together.

Clearly, though, writing for children makes other demands on authors. The genre is fraught with things you *need* to know and we will go through all of these.

The children's literature critic and writer Peter Hunt – if you have done any critical reading on children's literature you are sure to have come across his name and I recommend you read some of his work – found out to his cost that a controlled 'novel-writing' exercise, ignoring certain rules and bucking trends, led him to write a novel of his own choosing but one which also presented problems. He did his research and, based on his critical work, he was sure his novel was appropriate for the audience being addressed, telling them things they needed to know. But however carefully thought out and well intentioned the writing was, it did not necessarily mean the end result was generally acceptable to a publisher. Despite his extensive effort, Peter Hunt goes on to reveal that he rewrote the whole 75,000-word novel on the say so of his publisher.[4] Despite his careful marshalling of his text, his admission of defeat is entirely appropriate when faced with the critique of his editor. And you, too, must decide on this issue. How much are you prepared to rewrite, edit, scrap, on the advice of a third party? I once wrote a wonderful market scene: it had the rich smell of spikenards, herbs and spices from the Orient, sweet Cretan honey, ripe pineapples, grapes and oranges, fat juicy olives, garlic, bell peppers and tomatoes. My editor at that time, Ruth McCurry at Cassell, suggested we change the scene to 'clucking chickens'! And she was right, too.

The phrase 'generally acceptable' above, though, is a loaded one. Robert Leeson in an analogy between the writer and the storyteller, tells us that in the process of storytelling, 'you match story to audience, as far as you can' (Leeson 1985: 161) The caveat 'as far as you can' reveals indeterminate parameters. Peter Hunt's novel did what he wanted it to do and said what he wanted to say but, in his publisher's estimation, not necessarily what its readers would want to read. In a publishing industry-led world, certain unwritten rules for the writer exist to address this very issue. I will discuss as many as I know, as far as I can. I don't know everything (no one can) and the rules are unwritten, fluid and different for different publishers, writers, agents and so on. Other issues and ideas will similarly be addressed throughout the book. Through studying writing for children and critiquing work written for children, the unwritten rule book will be scrutinised.

While all rules are there to be broken, and the first fifty or so pages of J.K. Rowling's now legendary *Harry Potter and the Philosopher's Stone* breaks a number of them (thank goodness), knowing how and why the rules have been broken can be approached with knowledge rather than through serendipitous writing. Paul Klee only drew a line and took it for a walk *after* he had learned and understood his craft. Although, that's not to say serendipity has no part to play in the creative process. How often have all of us found our story leading us, rather than the other way round? This book will not ask you to ignore this, but help you to learn how to recognise, understand and use the creativity meaningfully. Further, if you have wandered off the track, hopefully you will be able to spot this and get back on course. All too often I have seen the story go down the wrong route and turn into a swamp. Writing is all about combining the inspiration with the craft, and I will be addressing this too, because the worst thing you can ever do is write in a formulaic manner. *Be original and interesting.* This book is not about discouraging creativity; rather, it is about recognising the best of your creativity.

You have to be aware of language.

Literary language, the language of the writer, narrative, with its verbs and nouns, metaphors and metonyms, similes, images, adjectives, adverbs, pronouns, syntax, synecdoche, codicils, silences as hypothetical postulates, truths and lies and endless ellipses . . . is a daunting prospect at any age. Yet using it is easier than you might think because it is what you deal with every day of your life. But when writing for children you also have to be aware of the appropriateness of language. I don't mean policing profanities (sometimes a well-timed curse is essential), but being aware of the audience we are addressing. A cliché may come as a breath of fresh air to some children (although personally I try to avoid them like the plague), but the development and delivery of metaphor and simile, for example, are not so straightforward.

The same goes for viewpoint. There is little point in knowing that the third-person viewpoint is a grammatical category of pronouns and verbs that is used when referring to objects or individuals other than the speaker and his or her addressee if you cannot use it objectively and with good purpose. And certainly there is no point in knowing this if you didn't understand what I wrote in the first place. Once again, don't worry, this will become clearer. When you see third-person narrative incorporating, say, a persuasively limited POV you will realise how an ordinary piece of text can suddenly come alive and you will be surprised how much you already know.

In many respects, this is why I am not a huge fan of many 'How to write . . . So you want to be a writer . . . ' books. Most of them discuss the mechanics of writing, the techniques, reflections, process, creativity and even inspiration but then miss the point of why we write and what we do with language.

It doesn't take a genius to tell you reading more helps you to write better.

'A.S. Byatt, in a discussion after a reading of her book *Angels and Insects* [Muswell Hill Bookshop, London, 1992], said that, for her, reading and writing were parts of the same process, that reading and writing are inseparable.'[5] Reading *what* and *whom* is crucial here. Antonia Byatt is an academic as well as an accomplished writer and I am sure she was not referring to reading 'how to write books'. My advice is that you should read wider and critically. Broaden your knowledge; this is not a one-stop tell-all book. No book can be and any that claims that status is already lying to you.

Implicitly, Byatt is referring to the acquisition and dissemination of knowledge. While Jacques Derrida claimed that writing is a slave in the service of knowledge, I would rather view it as the representation of experience. The esteemed American novelist Don DeLillo, in a rare interview, said that he wrote to find out how much he knew, where the act of writing was a form of thought. There is something very persuasive in this idea; especially if what we know is worth passing on. As James Friel has written:

> Reading is the best source of inspiration, the best means to educate yourself, to witness the skill of others – and to witness their disasters. It is through reading you learn to structure a tale, describe character, delineate action, judge what works and what, for you, does not . . . When you write, you are involving yourself in an enormous conversation with everyone else who has done likewise:

you learn from them, correct in your own work what you dislike in the works of others, pay tribute to work you admire, establish yourself in a tradition.

(Friel 2000: 27)

And, of course, what is a story if it is not the living trace of our past experience informing the future in present tense. *Homo fabula*, we are a storytelling species. From stories we gain pleasure but also advice, information, history and experience.

The acquisition and dissemination of the critically creative and the creatively critical experience become the sustenance that feeds the creative writer's reading and writing diet. They are the weft and warp of the cloth that eventually reveals the tapestry's narrative.

The writer benefits from critical understanding. Knowing how to analyse and being able to analyse what you are writing, or how and why what you have written can be improved, instead of hoping for the best, are so important to the craft of writing itself.

Writing is the critical representation of experience.

The idea that a representation of reality, created in any form, such as a novel or a film, could be transferred from the real to the represented without change is fantasy. It is a representation, never a precise replication. The representation is in itself an experience, but it does not replace the true experience. It merely sits alongside it as another experience. The book is the medium through which the writer's experience is translated into a story. Thus, it mediates the transference of the experience of the writer to the reader as another experience. Nevertheless, a critical representation of experience has to be the target of the writer. Why would anyone choose to provide a substandard version? What would be the point of that representation? A good story is not only something that is worth telling; it is something we all desire as readers, especially when it is told or written well. And that desire has no age barrier!

All writing is crucial to experience and, to paraphrase Ariel Dorfmann, it should rub against the grain; strike a chord; ring a bell to use another cliché. In essence it should make the reader think. And that is all the more reason why the writer shouldn't write without thinking, too.

To run with the grain is merely entertainment. And while we all need to be entertained at some times in our life, ask yourself this: is that all we need from writing? Is that all you would expect a child, or indeed anyone, to get from your writing? Is experience, which is so implicit to storytelling, to be sacrificed for entertainment alone? If you plan to read on from here, it is because you agree it is not.

The story as consumer- or commodity-led entertainment product is surely not a secure replacement for authentic experience. The potential for nurtured experience through story is implicit. It is one of the main purposes of storytelling and I share Walter Benjamin's wise notion that real storytellers share the wisdom of their experience. All of us, even the twenty-first century's technologically aware storytellers, working in the televisual or electronic medium, should not ignore this edict. Not as a didactic, I know better than you decree but as a shared experience, which joins the circulation of knowledge. For example, two of the best writers I have ever read are Sigmund Freud and Charles Darwin. Both of them would probably have made wonderful novelists, had they been so inclined. They were certainly very good storytellers. Yet I have read some bestselling novelists who can't tell a story.

Nevertheless, we still need to address the commodity issue. For all that it is an art, writing sells, it is a product, it is merchandise. Whether we like it or not we live in a commodity culture and living is expensive, but that does not mean all writing may as well be consigned to the shopping trolley of the commodity fetish. Jean Baudrillard might have already conceded that 'the commodity form is the first great medium of the modern world . . . [where] the message that the objects deliver through it is already extremely simplified, and it is always the same: their exchange value. Thus at bottom the message already no longer exists; it is the medium that imposes itself in its pure circulation' (Baudrillard 1985: 131), but a recent straw poll of my student writers rejected this notion when I asked them about their own writing. Most said they would write for nothing at all and money was not the consideration. What is important to them is the story.

I go along with this but there are few writers who do not desire publication or an audience of some sort. Nor can we forget that writing has become a massive industry. Publishing is consumer driven and thrives on the reproduction of what we write. If writers are to feed that industry is it not better that we do it with a critical awareness of what it is we are doing?

In this respect, few of us really needed Jack Zipes to remind us that certain writing, like the Disney adaptation of *Winnie the Pooh*, targeted at children,[6] is a simple device to 'hook children as consumers not because they believe their films have artistic merit and contribute to children's cultural development, but because they wanted to control children's aesthetic interests and consumer tastes' (Zipes 1997: 91). Zipes is often outspoken and not always right in his polemics, and he certainly got the story of the *Harry Potter* series wrong, but he is still a very astute reader of story and story experience and you should not dismiss this. Story-told experience is being sold in the same way that hamburger chains tie in products to promote their outlets. They are not thinking about nutritional value, but about ways of dragging people off the streets to spend their money.

Once again, then, while writing for children is not practice for writing for grown-ups, you must address your motives for writing. I have taught creative writing and I have lectured at creative-writing conferences, and the urge to publish is huge, but in doing so you have to regard the impressionability of your audience. However, forming the urge to publish into a disciplined, critical perspective is problematic, and you, as a prospective writer, will be encouraged throughout this book to address this issue. The craft of writing, the construction of a literary piece, the narrative strategies in a good, well-told story are often avoided by literary and critical theorists who preside over literature degrees in universities and colleges all over the world. This is already beginning to change – and by reading this book you might be a student already engaged in the change. Parts of this book will aim to help the change. As well as advising you how to write for children, I will be explaining critical strategies alongside the things you need to know. In my view there is no line, no gap, no border between the critical and the creative. They are both about addressing the representation of life experience. While it is considered that one looks back at works written and the other looks forward to production, both have a common ground in addressing the experience being passed on. At the end of the book I have compiled a selective bibliography which should help you to address this more clearly. Like all bibliographies, it is not a definitive list, but a startting point. *Get to know your subject.* In this sense you are advised to think of yourself as critically creative.

No one can tell you how to write!

This should be pinned on your wall. All we are able to do is help you to develop the craft and help you to understand what it is you are doing.

The craftsman or craftswoman has earned the right to be considered as an authority who is in control of the skill in which he or she has chosen to work. This means knowing as much as there is to know about that craft. While you may feel the mention of distinguished critics, such as Sigmund Freud or Jacques Derrida, never mind their works, has no relevance in a book on creative writing, especially one on writing for children, this should not be the case. Critical enquiry is a big part of creativity.

When, for example, Freud discusses issues related to writing, like *Unheimlich*, or Derrida leads us critically through traces of history in what we write today, our understanding of what they are thinking and writing can be usefully employed. After all, they are only carrying on a tradition which might be said to date back twenty-four centuries, to Aristotle's *Poetics*. The art of storytelling is not a secret and we have much to learn from those who have spent their lives writing about it. Not as a prescription to cure all ills but as a supplement to a vital diet. So critical-theoretical issues are liberally included in this book to help you to make sense of what it is you are writing.

In a parody of Karl Marx (another name that shouldn't scare you off) and with a backward glance at Aristotle's *Poetics*, it has been suggested that the aim of criticism is to 'describe writing' and the purpose of the poetics of writing is to 'change it'.[7]

I can see the sense of this statement. Especially in the case being made for poetics by the writer concerned. But I also feel the separation between the 'criticism' and 'poetics' is too simple a proposition. We cannot simply forget about the creative in the critical or vice versa. Their narratives are too intertwined. But in recognising this part of my aim in this book will be to reveal that we can combine critical and creative strategies to the advantage of writing. Thus, this is not just a book on 'how to write for children'; it also addresses a critical analysis of writing, the theoretical tool that you can bring to your own work. It is a book that promotes the combination of both critical and creative strategies and addresses story from a critically creative perspective – with an academic perspective, from someone who also writes. Hence the use of the term 'creative vigilance',[8] which I will invoke from time to time.

I have split the book into four distinct chapters. After this perspective on crafting the other sections are 'Write the rights/know the wrongs', 'Write the height', 'Write the rest'. Incorporated into this is the 'Pyramid plot structure'. This serves as a diagrammatic plot model, which is also an analysing tool and even serves as an *aide-mémoire*.

The secret to writing is there is no secret, but you do have to work at the craft. Learning to write for children is about hard work. This book does not present a magic formula, because there is no such thing. But if you have managed to read this far without being frightened off, let me now lead you into the magical, labyrinthine world of writing for children, with a critical perspective.

Writing should be fun and enjoyable. We have anxious moments about words and phrases, plots and stories. We struggle to say what we mean and write what we think, but if we cannot deliver a book worth reading, frankly we do not deserve to be published. This book addresses many issues, use it to try to make your own book a good one. If this book helps to produce a single worthwhile book for children I will have succeeded.

Forgive the hyperbole and enjoy the experience.

Know the Wrong

2 Write the rights/ know the wrongs

This chapter is designed to set up the premise of the story about to unfold throughout the book. When I go on to address issues such as fiction, for example, you will need to be able to call on all of the information that follows. I have also given examples of what I am referring to, but you must try out your own, too (I will be reminding you of this throughout the book). There is nothing wrong with practising. You have to practise your craft. I have over forty writing credits and I am still practising. Philip Pullman once said he never wrote drafts, but he might write a dozen versions of the same story. The reason he gives for this is that each version has to be seen as a final version, not a draft, if it is to be taken as seriously as it merits. Everyone should read Pullman's *His Dark Materials* trilogy for themself. The point I am making here is: the minute we begin a new piece the new practice begins. Once you have practised on that you will have to practise on the next piece you begin because there is no such thing as the perfect piece of writing. And, of course, we all know there is no automatic right to publication.

In beginning each new story we are confronted with the same things, so it is *story* we begin with here.

Story

In reading this book you have already decided to write for children and you are looking for guidance. You probably already have a story and want to learn how to tell it well. Your reasons are immaterial. You will already have some idea of what kind of story you want to write.

Whether it is mystery, thriller, fantasy, science fiction, historical or whatever, the story will be germinating inside of you. One thing is certain – it will always be a *story*.

Story is the way all of us communicate the narrative of the events of our histories, everyday lives, dreams, projected fantasies and future hopes. It is the narrative of experience. Story, it could also be said, is the narrative of events. I would rather describe it as the narrative of wonder. If you have a wonderful story, then it should be told. But if it is not wonderful, why does it deserve to be told? Harsh as it may sound, you have to ask yourself this question. Importantly, you also have to remember *if you do not have a story you do not have a book to write*.

As Freud wrote, way back in the nineteenth century, 'the storyteller has a peculiar power over us; by means of the moods he can put us in to, he is able to guide the current of our emotions, to dam it up in one direction and to make it flow in another'[9] (Freud 1990: 375). But the storyteller is defined through the offered story. No matter how gifted, crafted and expert the writing, without a good story everything you write will have been in vain. Everything else is just the craft that brings the story to bear and you cannot write what does not exist. Writing without a story is like singing a song without a tune. It cannot be done.

A good story, said McKee (1999: 20), is 'something worth telling that the rest of the world wants to hear'. However simple the story is, it has to be stimulating. This is one of the first things you have to consider.

An accomplished story for children must have the same fundamental ingredients as a story for adults. Think about what you like to read before you even begin writing. Then think again about what draws you to the story. For example, it will almost certainly be the main character who interests you most. It is the characters and their development, not plot, which keep us interested. Do you have a character for your story or a story about a character?

Assuming you do, then, in its most basic form, a story can be broken down into six elements: balance, disharmony, inciting incident, problem, resolution and consequence.

- *Balance* All is well at home; nothing particularly interesting is going on.

- *Disharmony* Suddenly the mood changes (for good or ill).
- *Inciting incident* Just when things were looking better a change of mood provokes a change to something 'other'.
- *Problem* There is now an even more serious dilemma that needs resolving.
- *Resolution* The story can be brought to a conclusion.
- *Outcome* The outcome/effect/conclusion/reward/purpose of the story unfolds as it comes to the end.

This will be set out as follows:

- *Beginning* Meet the main character(s) and introduce the problem.
- *Middle* Focus on the problem, which gets worse through the inciting incident – introduce a focus of resistance such as suspense/surprise/ tension.
- *End* Resolve the problem, whichever way, then get out as quickly as possible.

Crucial to this is the understanding that balance, disharmony and the inciting incident can all happen on the first page. If your story begins with an immediate crisis, all this suggests is that prior to this there was balance – if not, why start your story later? For example, 'Josie heard a noise' is a pretty good opener because it begs investigation and therein begins the story. The never-mentioned balance is introduced to disharmony and as Josie goes to investigate we can expect an inciting incident, whereupon the story continues.

Aristotle said the most important thing in any story is the sequence of events. Each event has a cause and effect, and each is connected in the plot. We can see this idea of a series of events as six stages of plot development:

- The opening
- The arrival of conflict
- The early achievement
- The twist and change
- The denouement
- The final outcome

It is often suggested that a story for children should open with conflict. Don't delay the conflict's introduction too long. This is not a rigid structure but, as you can see, crucially there has to be *change*. By the end something has to have changed from the beginning: things never go back to being exactly the same as they were. As we can see from the plot model, six changes are identified as progressive. But don't take my headings as gospel: try out your own and see what works for you.

The characters must be seen to change from the beginning, through the middle to the end. The cliché 'he never changes' simply does not hold true. We all change; real life is about change.

A story has to change, respond to change and create change, especially for the story's leading characters, through whom the story is told. Certainly, in children's fiction, each chapter should be a story in its own right, with its own beginning, middle and end. Although what you must remember is that each chapter should bring a meaningful change to the life of your main character(s). If your story isn't doing this, then you are not moving the story forward when you should be. A golden rule in writing for children is that the story has to progress. Don't dally on insignificant issues or subplots that hamper progress. I will develop these issues later when I look at the pyramid plot structure, where I will also reveal how to keep the story moving forward quickly and in an interesting fashion.

There will, of course, be slight variations on the model I have shown above, which will be addressed below. However, it is a good model to work from for stories for children. It works for picture books all the way through to fiction for the oldest age group.

We are all capable of reading a story idea, then thinking we could do it better. We are also able to take some hackneyed ideas and rehash them with the view that we can make them better – in a contemporary setting, say. To beg, borrow, parody or flirt with another's story (however good or bad) is only going to end in clichéd predictability unless it is handled with great care. You still have to do the work. Besides, you do have your own stories to tell; you just have to get used to accessing them.

In considering this, let me introduce you to something I found interesting. In 'Creative Writers and Day Dreaming' (Freud 1990: 129), Freud declares that

We laymen have always been intensely curious to know . . . from what source that strange being, the creative writer, draws his material, and how he manages to make such an impression on us with it and to arouse in us emotions of which, perhaps, we had not even thought ourselves capable.

He concludes that nothing the creative writier produces will 'make creative writers of us'. What Freud points us to is an opinion that we ought to be able to discover the answer in ourselves. What he adds to this is most interesting for writers for children, though:

Should we not look for traces of imaginative activity as early as in childhood? . . . Might we not say that every child at play behaves like a creative writer, in that he creates a world of his own, or, rather, rearranges the things of his world in a new way, which pleases him. It would be wrong to think he does not take life seriously and he expends large amounts of emotion on it . . . The creative writer does the same as a child at play. He creates a world of fantasy which he takes very seriously – that is, which he invests with large amounts of emotion – while separating it sharply from reality. *Language has preserved this relationship between children's play and poetic creation.*

(*Ibid.*: 131–2; my emphasis)

Freud makes it easy for us to agree with him. Indeed, his old friend Carl Jung agrees when he says the creation of something new is not accomplished by the intellect alone but by the play instinct. The creative mind plays with the object it loves. The creative imagination, the instinct of *play*, is something we all have, only we repressed it as childish when confronted by the adult world. This does not mean it is gone for ever. What you have to do is seek a way of releasing it for yourself. What is called for is a kind of soul-mining, where you seek to excavate the playful stories that have become buried somewhere inside of you. But first of all you have to exercise your surveying skills. In your soul-mining: there is no point in sinking shafts and digging great holes willy-nilly: you will just end up getting lost in the dark. Rather, take time to look around and survey the terrain. Get to know where the best story is located.

From small acorns . . .

Albert Einstein once said that imagination is more important than knowledge. Unfortunately, however, all too often we have insufficient knowledge to acknowledge what is truly inspirational in our imagination. Inspiration, too, is often cited as the source of many good stories and every story needs a little magic, which inspiration brings. But you will find *awareness* is the most inspiring element of the writer's tool kit. Be aware; stay alert to the possibilities. Don't close your mind to even the smallest trace of a story. It is often the small ideas that bring big stories. The stories are all around, waiting to be written, so stay creatively vigilant. When asked once how he wrote so many songs, Bob Dylan replied that they were all around, in the air, all you had to do was reach up and pluck them. Harvesting the fruit is just another version of soul-mining. You have to listen for stories others cannot hear. But if you do not tune-in in the first place, how can you expect to hear them?

For example, here is a true incident. In my street there is a kid called Joe (he's twenty-four now but since I've known him for fifteen years he's still a kid to me). He's a filmmaker now and I recently saw him working on a new project in his garden. While he was directing, I spotted another documentary film crew filming Joe filming; it was for their student dissertation. Suddenly Joe waved across the garden and turned the camera on me. I was watching the crew filming Joe who was filming me. Of course I smiled and waved back. Not awe-struck (or star-struck), I've been on film sets before. But when I was watching the documentary crew watching Joe watching me a creative trinity was completed. I had made a connection.

If the filming incident had happened to me when I was thirteen it would have been magic because filming fascinates me. I would have been keen to get involved. Therein lay a story. It came instantly. All I had to do was take myself back to a time when I would have been in awe of what was going on.

It isn't magic. It's all about being imaginative and alert to the possibilities. Hopefully the story *will* be magic, though. It is called *Shooting Joe*.[10] Consider it:

> Josie is thirteen and in love with Joe, which is always going to have
> an unlikely outcome. She decides that the only way forward in

their relationship is for her to get a part in his film. She succeeds but tragedy befalls Josie's plans when Joe's girlfriend comes down from university to play the leading role and Josie . . .

You get the drift, though you might be forgiven for saying not everyone is lucky enough to catch a film being made in their next-door neighbour's back garden to stimulate inspiration.

True. Except, I lied (that's allowed). The story is not true!

Joe does indeed live in my street, and he wants to be a filmmaker . . . the rest I made up. He wasn't in the garden, there was no student documentary being shot at the same time and as for Josie, she's a figment of my imagination, although I can remember being thirteen (just about).

As I sat at my desk writing this book, the entire story of Josie and Joe came to me in one of those writer's lacunas that you will all recognise. Freud called it daydreaming. It came straight off the top of my head, through a series of consequential thoughts connecting Joe to an awestruck teenager. I won't let the story go away, though. I plan to revisit it throughout this book. Josie and Joe are not done yet!

Story is the narrative of experience: your experience

Homo fabula, homo historia, we are story, story is us. We communicate and experience life through stories every day of our lives. Writing a story, then, is the archaeological dig that reveals the narrative of its own truths, its own history, culture and prospective future. Not the mysteries of writing but the magic and mysteries of life. When we write stories we are not just digging up old, dead metaphorical bones. The dig is part of the story. The dig is also part of the stories of your life, which you are digging up. As Sophocles says so eloquently, look and you will find it. What is unsought will go undetected. Get your fingers dirty and start unearthing all the stories that you know exist.

As storytellers, we are resurrecting the narrative of the once living that can get lost and forgotten on the road of historical dismantling. As Jacques Derrida would go on to explain, it is the lost and forgotten that interest us here. For surely the unsuccessful repression of any story retains a certain legibility which limits its own historical opaqueness?[11]

Those repressed and perplexing narratives looking for a voice to remain with us are the real stories. The clues to a story are everywhere to be seen, if you look. Don't let yours go the way of the dinosaurs.

The archaeology metaphor has just reminded me of something else. I had a very good student once, who graduated with a Master's degree with distinction. She was writing a novel about a group of children whose parents were archaeologists. The basic plot was that every year, come their summer holidays, the kids were whisked off to a dig somewhere exotic. The world of Aztecs, Incas, Pompeii all beckoned, yet they hated it. They wanted to be on a beach somewhere, chilling out and doing teenage things. Since we had an archaeology department in the college, which organised weekend digs, I asked the student if she wanted to join them on one. The suggestion was that it might be good for background research.

'What, with these nails?' she replied, holding up her hands to show ten neatly manicured, highly polished, bright red nails.

You can interpret this story in many ways. For instance, you might be critical that she was writing a story without proper research. But that's not quite what I am getting at. The line 'What, with these nails?' appeared in her book. Indeed, it became a crucial turning point. Her central character was a very reluctant archaeologist and the complete antithesis of her earthy parents. Her story was about a teenage girl with nails and an appearance to care for. The fictional teenage girl was banished to boarding school while her parents worked the sites of the world and her life was all about growing up and girlish things, shared with like-minded girls enclosed in dorms. My student knew exactly why the whole dig business would be her character's biggest nightmare. The story wasn't about an archaeological dig but about avoiding it. She saw a lot of herself in her leading character, but, as you can see, that too is a story. And it leads us nicely to the next item, characters (you might wonder if I planned that).

Characters

It is characters that interest us most when we read fiction. It is characters we come to love, hate, laugh at, cry at and empathise with. They are endearing, charming, abhorrent, enjoyable, strange, creepy, curious, good, bad, evil, cute, happy, sad, indifferent, objectionable, domineering, subordinate, bullies, bullied, boys, girls, men, women, rabbits, frogs, Teddy bears, dogs, black, Asian, Scottish (like me), fair, spotty, freckled, pretty, pretty useless, my little sister, athletic, silly, funny, snooty, political animals, monsters, machines, robots, mermaids . . . the list is endless. But they are never bland! So repeat it like a mantra! It is characters that interest us most when we read fiction. Everything else is just there for support in their development.

In the archaeology story I related above we can see it is the character who provides the premise for the piece. It was easy to encourage the student with the red nails to construct her leading character. All she had to do was construct a younger version of herself. She knew everything she did not want to know about archaeology and knew how to go about avoiding it. After all, she had spent her life avoiding such situations.

Let's look at character in more depth.

The first decision you have to make is what you want your character to be. Whether it is a monkey or a man matters not if the character is to take on an anthropomorphic story that your child reader can recognise. What *is* important is wanting your character to be someone of interest whom you can take forward. Bring it to the fore and let it stand in the spotlight. Often it's the early introduction of a character which reveals whether he or she is ready for development, or indeed strong enough to carry the story.

In the section on story, above, I introduced Josie as a thirteen-year-old girl who fancies Joe. The introduction told us virtually nothing at all. A character needs to be introduced in relation to its surroundings, emotional state, level of maturity, sense of development and experience, and most importantly as a three-dimensional, believably real person. Let's look at a couple of examples of Josie by mapping out a couple of introductions to her.

Example one

> Her dad was shaking his head emphatically. 'No you can't have your belly button pierced!'
>
> Josie frowned back at him, 'Rachel and Amina had it done

yesterday!' She really wanted to shout out, *Mum would have let me! You never let me do anything.* But that would have been cruel.

'Come on, Jojo,' sighed her dad. 'You're only thirteen.'

Josie hated being called Jojo these days and how could anyone be only thirteen? Her mum would have understood.

Josie tugged at her hair in frustration. She felt like cutting it all off! That would teach him. Except Joe liked her long hair too. And life would be miserable without Joe.

She fought back her tears. 'You treat me like I'm still a little girl!'

What we understand about Josie from this short passage is immediately apparent:

- Parental conflict
- Style consciousness
- A wish to be one of the gang
- A wistful longing for a missing mother
- Josie's age is thirteen
- No one understands (except perhaps Rachel and Amina)
- Josie has long hair
- Her dad and Joe like her long hair
- Her nickname is Jojo
- Perhaps Dad still sees Jojo as his little girl
- Josie would like to punish her dad by cutting off her hair
- Perhaps she is rebelling because of her missing mother
- Josie likes Joe
- Joe is the only thing worth living for
- Dad doesn't know he has a 'teenager in love'
- Dad forgets what it is like to be a teenager
- Josie's growing up

Thus, each topic can be developed as a separate strand as the story pans out and there is much to play with when developing Josie. But let's take a different tack.

Example two

> Josie stared at the doctor. He was opening and closing his mouth like a fish. It made him look stupid and she should have laughed. Except it wasn't funny.
>
> He shone a light into her eye and that made her head hurt. Then he opened and shut his mouth again.
>
> She couldn't hear him saying, 'Josie, can you hear me?'
>
> She couldn't hear anything except her own thoughts.
>
> The words 'hello, teenager' echoed round and round in her brain. It was the last thing she remembered hearing out loud. That was two days ago. Joe will never want her now!

As you can see, this gives us a completely different story. Yet we learn much about Josie again.

However, there is much more to know about Josie at this age if we are to create a fully rounded character, rather than a caricature. In her own mind she is fully into puberty, like Thomas Hardy's Tess, 'estimated a woman . . . not more than a child'. And while we only need to *reveal* what is relevant, appropriate and usable we need to *know* everything about her. If the fact that she has breasts is not relevant to the story, how appropriate is their mention? We already know she is on the cusp of adulthood, so her physical development will be important to her (and therefore to you as the writer). It will affect her view of selfhood, her moods, how others perceive her. If twenty-four-year-old Joe was happy to tuck her up in bed when he babysat for her ten years ago (when he was fourteen and she was three), how does he or she feel about that now? The target audience is crucial here, too. What Nabokov found appropriate in the formation of Lolita may not be appropriate in Josie, but her development is. It is all about getting to know who your character is.

By the way, a quick glance at the above introductions will tell you the approximate reading age is nine to eleven. On this issue of reading age, *the tip here is to let your audience read up*, to reach up and aspire to understand the generation immediately above them. That way writing about the experiences of an elder can generate the anticipation of these experiences which the reader might face in their own future. Children like to read about what they have not yet experienced.

Thus, the advice is get to know your characters. What makes characters real to the reader? What makes them believable? Why should we care about them? Do you care enough about your characters? When a friend of mine wrote a series of books, she was in love with her main character, whom she visualised as a young, tousled haired David Essex in his pop star and *That'll Be the Day* era. Which, of course, was a throwback to her own youth. It meant she could see her character in her mind's eye.

I could continue to explain Josie in different ways, but you need to do your own exercise. When you create a character you have to get to know how you can use it. But you might also like to consider this. When I was working on an animation series we had to create what is known as a 'bible'. It is a description of all the major characters, and as production starts the description is accompanied by pictures and relevant events that can be drawn on. For example, if Josie loses her mother in episode two, we have to think about continuity for the remaining episodes. Bearing in mind the number of people who work on films, the bible is an essential *aide-mémoire*

Let's look at a mock-up of Josie's bible entry:

> Josie (age thirteen); nickname Jojo; only child; five foot tall and growing; slim; long fair hair; bright blue eyes; best friends Rachel and Amina; sits at the edge of the gang, not quite fully integrated, wants to ingratiate herself and be popular; in love with Joe who used to be her babysitter; mother dead; father struggling to cope with life; she's sad and confused and essentially lonely; she likes pizza and fish but definitely no meat; she reads a lot; doesn't care for TV . . .

The point is to sort out as much information as you can so that you can get to know what makes your character. Even if you are not going to use all of the information, this exercise helps to create historical depth which you can draw on to create a more three-dimensional character, rather than settling for a flat caricature. Make your characters tall, rich, short, fat, thin, muscle bound, intellectual, sexy, bald, northern, foreign, poor, black, gay, white . . . Give them clothes, jewels, cars, houses . . . Give them personalities.

Put yourself in this situation, though. When I meet new people they invariably ask me what I do. When I speak they recognise where I'm from (Scotland). They see how I am dressed, if I am shaved, know if I smell – and what of, good or bad. What they are doing, even from first impressions, is piecing together a polysemic picture of me for their own satisfaction (this doesn't always have to be favourable). To others, our personalities are a set of clues. This is what you have to do with your characters. Make them whole; make them real; make them people – even if they are rabbits, fish or tank engines. Then once you have a sense of their past and present try to anticipate their hopes for the future. Figure out where you want to take them and how you want them to develop, *but give them room to breathe*.

Let your character mature slowly. The 'facts' you have assembled for yourself are not constraints but marks, traces, footprints, signs, hints, shadows, silhouettes and insinuations about a person. Leak the clues deliberately and at a good pace. If he or she deviates from the ideal model in your early assessment it is because your character is developing with the story – and this is crucial to any story. His or her eventual personality will evolve from the figure you see in your mind's eye. That's not to say going in completely blind is advisable, though.

Think about the character you want to write about then create a short narrative that includes who he or she is. Think about what defines them, where they stand in relation to:

- The story world at large[12]
- The context of the story
- What might be going on in her head
- What might be going on in the head of others close to her
- What might be real and what might be imagined
- Where they might be going.

Also, try to think about the things that I did not say when I introduced Josie. Surely it is patronising the reader even to report the fact that the second portrait of Josie reveals she is deaf. However, I did leak some clues. And if you missed them go back and read them again: they do exist.

Show not tell

Clearly, *show not tell* is the operative phrase here. Show your readers your characters, parade them down the catwalk of your narrative, let them sparkle and let the reader gasp in wonder at the way they have been dressed for them. Take care of them and they will take care of you. Let me *tell* you a little story.

A friend of mine is a talented sculptor and once he was commissioned to work on a public exhibition. He had to sculpt a life-sized model of a boy from a solid piece of stone. It was to be undertaken in full view of the public so they could see the work taking place. Day in and day out the people of the town would stop and inspect and have a look and give advice, but my friend's attention was drawn to one young child. Every day the same child, he was about six or seven, walked to school and on the way he would only give the sculpture the briefest of glances as he passed. Day after day, as he chipped away, the sculptor tried to attract his attention. He shouted to the boy and showed off his work but the boy showed no interest, no curiosity at all. It was like the sculpture was just another landmark on the journey to be taken for granted. This worried the sculptor a little. After all, he was supposed to be presenting a sculpture of a boy and yet this real boy showed no interest.

Then, one day, just as the sculptor thought he was finished, something happened. Before the final unveiling, when the sculptor was giving the sculpture its last rub down, the boy finally stopped to take a look. He pondered the stone boy for a moment, then a bright, wide smile crossed his face.

'That's magic,' said the boy to the sculptor. 'How did you know he was in there?'

My friend the sculptor was cock-a-hoop. At last his sculpture had become tangible and real.

Is this story true? Do you care? The point is that creating a character is like this. You begin with a block then chip away and chip away, until he or she emerges to become real. Just as the sculpted boy became real for the little boy, so too did the little boy in my story, who had ignored the sculptor all this time, eventually become real for you – and you didn't even realise I was drawing you in, did you?

But consider something else here. The boy had no relationship with the sculptor at first. There was no dialogue between them until the second boy, the stone one, appeared. A third person, if you like, and this is something we will consider when we come to dialogue. A relationship between two people, in this case the sculptor and the boy, often needs a MacGuffin[13] to relay the story between them; in this case the stone boy. The third element becomes the catalyst for change. I will explain this more when we look at dialogue (usually the best way to introduce a MacGuffin – although it can be anything really, from a telephone to a stone boy who never speaks, at least to us cynical old adults).

Finally, then, once you have made your characters real, you must make them come alive. They have to fly off the page. Even if you don't like their characteristics, you have to love your characters; they are crafted from your modelling clay, nurtured from your soul, so give them blood, sweat and tears, laughter, struggle and achievements; give them opinions and arguments; give them crisis and conclusion; give them actions and reactions; give them good cause and effect; give them love. Chip away all the dead weight to reveal their souls. Give them the gift of life! It's not magic, it's craft.

Viewpoint

After you have decided on your story, easily one of the most important decisions you will ever make when you begin writing, then, concerns viewpoint.

Who is going to tell the story?

Through whose eyes are we told the story?

How is the story to be told?

Where does the narrator stand in relation to the other characters in the story?

It is crucial that you answer these questions. Then, once you have decided on the viewpoint, you must stick to it. Once children begin hearing or reading a story, they become absorbed by a central voice. Your reader may even *become* that character so it's important to understand its power. At least when writing for the early years changing that narrative voice only leads to confusion (moving into teenage fiction gives some scope for multiple voices, although you are advised not to use more than a couple here, either).

Choose your viewpoint carefully. You are not only choosing for yourself, but for the reader, and your child reader has high expectations. Having persuaded them to pick up your book, it would be a shame to let the reader down by avoidable sloppiness in delivery.

Viewpoint always comes under two clear headings: *objective* and *subjective*.

Objective

In most literature, never mind children's the opportunity to use objective viewpoint, often referred to as 'second person' is slight, because it relies on a style of reporting in which the narrator stays outside the characters at all times. The most prominent examples are those narratives that address 'you' directly, like much of this book. But it's not all instructions on how to operate the washing machine. It can be used as a fictional form. For example:

> She didn't look like any kind of thief but Josie picked up the shiny stone, put it in her pocket and then ran down the road. Joe walked steadily behind her. At her front gate Josie looked over her shoulder before going inside the house. Once inside she ran to the window. Joe walked by without even glancing in. She pulled the curtains shut and sighed. Josie didn't look like the kind of girl who would have something to hide. But then who does?

The question 'But then who does?' ensures the narrator is keeping well out of the character all the time. We do not get any sense of what either Josie or Joe is feeling or thinking. Why did she pick up the stone? What did she want it for? Why did she run down the road? Why did she look back? We are given no clues. The only question comes from the unknown narrator. We can guess Joe has something to do with Josie's actions. We can guess Josie is perhaps nervous of seeing Joe, but we don't *know* and thus it is an entirely unsuitable choice for young fiction. The narrative stays on the surface. It doesn't explore the emotional depth, or subjectivity, of the character. Nevertheless, you can never write it off as it does have its uses, especially in early reading and picture books.

In certain picture books the objective viewpoint can be used to great effect because, while the story is reported, the picture fills in the subtext. This is also especially useful when you are trying to mediate between the reader and the child.

Jasper's Beanstalk, by Nick Butterworth and Mick Inkpen, is a perfect example. On the first page the text reads, 'On Monday Jasper found a bean.' A picture of a smiling Jasper accompanies this on the facing page: he is holding up the bean. The viewpoint of the narrative is 'reported' while the happy picture interprets and conveys the emotion or, we might say, the 'subjective state' of Jasper. He is smiling and clearly happy with his find. It is this semiotic combination of narrative and illustrated viewpoints which engages the child as the reader takes on the reporter's role. The book mediates between the 'objective reporting' and the 'subjective picture' being conveyed. But the list is endless. Go and read them!

I will discuss books like this at greater length as we proceed, but we can immediately see the benefit of such a narrative in a read-to/beginner's reading book.

Obviously, the collaboration between author and illustrator is crucial to the overall picture, but if you have a good idea, setting up an exercise is easy. Bear in mind, though, the picture and text can be contradictory. The child is already beginning to read the paradoxes of representation.[14] For example, take these double-page spreads:

Page 1	Text:	(blank)
	Picture:	(*Ben is smiling as he looks at a cardboard box.*)
Page 2	Text:	It's only an old cardboard box, Ben.
Page 3	Text:	Beep! Beep!
	Picture:	(*Ben is sitting in the box. He is dressed as a racing driver in his car.*)
Page 4	Text:	Did you win the race, Ben?

It's only an old cardboard box is reported by the objective view of the narrator. But through the illustrator's pictures the narrator/reader soon learns what Ben can see and how he feels about it.

In the section on picture books we will look at other variations, but, as you can see, a viewpoint quite unsuited to prose fiction might be appropriate for your picture-book story. I will explain this in more detail later, too.

Another good use of this viewpoint comes in non-fiction, like this book, as I said before, where the reader is addressed as 'you'. As you can see, the personalising of the narrative allows me to address you directly, and this is entirely appropriate for a book of this kind.

Subjective

This is the most common viewpoint. The word 'subjective' equates to the internal thinking and interior emotional particulars of the character or subject. In short it gets inside the head of the character you are presenting.

It also comes with three useful headings – *omniscient, first person* and *third person* (which is really a limited version of *omniscient*).

Omniscient

This is the perspective of a divine, all-knowing, all-seeing view of the world. Everyone's thoughts, feelings, conversations, actions and setting are available for consumption; every scene is scrutinised and the author tells us everything there is to know. Popularised in the nineteenth century, when writers felt it necessary to give us the story of the whole society they were writing about, it is rarely if ever used now. Part of the reason for this is that the impersonal nature of the narrative makes it very intrusive and difficult for a reader to empathise with any character because the narrative is a mass of polyphonic voices, including the author's omniscient one. For example, here are Joe and Josie again:

> Although the moon sat brightly in the clear night sky, he couldn't see the mouse at the bottom of the garden as it scuttled out of sight. It was two in the morning and Joe shouldn't have been up. But it was warm and he couldn't sleep.
>
> Nearby, Josie watched him light a cigarette, wishing she knew what he was thinking. Even though she had known Joe all her life,

she hardly knew him at all. That didn't matter though. What mattered to Josie was being close to Joe.

Joe blew his cigarette smoke up at the moon and it made Josie smile.

Joe sucked on his cigarette again. He was looking forward to seeing Mary again. He'd felt bad about having to leave her in Durham but the film was nearly finished.

Josie watched the smoke curl in the moonlight. She was convinced Joe was thinking about her. As he stubbed the cigarette out and turned to go back inside, Josie ducked behind the curtain. 'Goodnight, sweet Joe,' she whispered. She was hoping he would look up. He didn't, though she was glad he didn't spot her either.

A couple of cats snarled at each other across the houses. The still silence was broken.

Funny getting that letter from Josie this morning, Joe thought. Before he went back to sleep he wondered if he should show it to Mary.

In her own bed, Josie held herself tightly and thought about nothing except Joe.

Back in Durham, under the gaze of the same moon, Mary smiled warmly at Kazuo before kissing him.

Another cat snarled.

Mary was thinking that tomorrow she and Joe had much to discuss. But tonight she had other things on her mind.

As for Kazuo . . .

While the result is worth the effort and I suggest you try it as an exercise, it is difficult to sustain. And the temptation to develop and lean towards the story of one character, rather than writing the others in tandem, is almost irresistible, even when the characters are intertwined. The problem is not quite so bad in the little triangle I created above, but the days of a Walter Scott panoply have been refined since then, and you have to be aware of this.

We can also see that the characters are only linked in pairs at this stage: Josie and Joe; Joe and Mary; Mary and Kazuo. Nevertheless, each pair sets its own trinity: Josie, Joe and Mary; Joe, Mary and Kazuo; and, eventually, Mary, Kazuo and Josie. The triangular association is important. Once again it is the third-person element that provides the MacGuffin for the story to proceed. In this case Mary is the MacGuffin in Josie's story, Kazuo is the MacGuffin in Joe's story and Josie is the MacGuffin in Kazuo's. So we are given the choice of divided loyalties, making it hard to empathise with one character. In looking at Joe and Josie we cannot presuppose that Mary does not deserve our empathy; and, of course, there is Kazuo to consider too.

First person

Enid Blyton never wrote for children in the first person because she thought they didn't like it. This is not true. As children, this is probably the first viewpoint with which we all identify. Even if we begin writing with what is essentially the objective viewpoint, we tend to develop the subjective through the first person.

Our first writing comes from the personal view, we think in the personal view. We address the world from a personal perspective when we are telling a story and when we are formulating our own stories. But in written form it is considered to be the hardest to maintain, especially when writing for children.

The advantages are manifest. Generally colloquial in nature, it brings about a sense of informality, setting up a cosy conversational relationship with the narrator. They are speaking directly to the reader, so this allows for feelings and introspection to be examined at a close level. Also, the narrator's perception of other characters is a lot easier to comprehend because gut reactions can be inserted without being intrusive. For example:

> 'Right, then. Ready to go out?'
> Oh my God! What on earth is she wearing? Has she any idea what she looks like? 'You look nice,' I lied. What else can I say? Sally's my best friend. I can't hurt her feelings, now can I?
> 'Come on, what's up?'
> 'Oh, nothing.'

There are several disadvantages to using this viewpoint. You rely entirely on a single, subjective view, only seeing the world from one angle. And, of course, we only get one set of emotions. After Sally (above) asks whether they are ready to go out, her best friend – the 'I' – as narrator doesn't know at this stage what she might be thinking. Here are Sally's thoughts: 'This'll test our friendship. If she can't tell me I look a prat in this she's not being honest, like we agreed.' We *can't* know this because we only get one viewpoint, although, presumably, all will be revealed as the book proceeds. But you can see how it sets up a problem. In the denouement the narrator reveals all:

'Sal, you mean you were only testing me?'

'Of course,' Sally replied.

Boy, do I feel a prat, now. Poor Sally, what must she think of me? 'I suppose I should have been honest with you?'

Sal just smiled back at me. Always the same effortless smile. I didn't deserve it.

'Come on,' she said. 'That's what mates are for.'

I knew she was right. 'I know you are right really. I just didn't want to hurt your feelings. After all, who can we turn to for honest opinions if not each other?'

Sally laughed. 'You need a hair cut.'

I frowned, then laughed too. 'Oh, you bitch! I know, it's a complete mess . . . I'm trying to grow it out.'

Of course, there's lots of fun to be had with this kind of misunderstanding, and you will also find it useful in stories where realism is a high priority.

Because the narrator addresses the reader directly, using the prefix 'I', the reader tends to be drawn into collusion with the narrator; like hearing the story being told by a best friend. The best example I have seen for children is without doubt Anne Fine's *Goggle Eyes*. For a lesson in sustained first-person storytelling I recommend you read it. When you do, you will find you are three pages into the book before you even realise the story is being told by Kitty Killin, who is as good a storyteller as Anne Fine is a writer. Therein you will see the power of creating a convincing storyteller. It is the intimacy of a real-life struggle, in the case of Kitty having to deal with Mum's new boyfriend, which draws us close to the character of Kitty. But we do so by eavesdropping as Kitty tells her story to her friend Helly, so that Helly can compare it with her own dilemma. The eavesdropping technique is simple but very effective. Find a captive audience, sit them down and then tell them your story, now where have I heard that one before? Read *Goggle Eyes*, you will not regret it. But don't think first person is just suitable for the older age group.

Tony Bradman's wonderful *Dilly the Dinosaur* series is also written in the first person, through the eyes of Dilly's sister, Dorla. It is a fine example of good, subtle, first-person narrative for the younger reader.

Third person

Often referred to as the 'limited omniscient', this viewpoint is by far the most popular in fiction. When writing for children, though, you must consider whether to use *third person unlimited* or *third person limited*. Both are appropriate, but once again *write the height* comes into play when making the decision.

THIRD PERSON UNLIMITED

About three-quarters of all adult novels are written from this viewpoint, which allows for a multiple perspective, revealing the 'subjectivity' of more than one character. In young fiction this is almost never used as children find the change in perspective confusing. They are being asked to imagine what it is like to be one character, then they have to change to being another. That's not to say it can't work, though. This is an extract from something I published some time ago (for ages seven to nine):

> 'Zak!' shouted Ben, as he held on to the sides of the speeding cart. 'Turn down the burned-out section of the merchant district.'
>
> 'You mean the place we nearly fried in,' replied Zakkai, recalling the time Nihilus almost burned them out using fireballs fired from a giant catapult.
>
> 'That's the place,' said Ben. 'Perhaps we can lose them in the narrow streets.'
>
> 'Here goes!'

As the cart whipped down the burned-out alleyways of the old merchant district, Justin looked over his shoulder, anxiously. 'Faster Zak, go faster! They are gaining on us.'

'Here I come!' cheered Capella. He was obviously enjoying himself.

Suddenly, Zak threw Justin the coil of rope that had lain at his side. 'Justin, quickly, the beam,' he said, pointing at a blackened building.

Justin needed no other advice. He could see the burned-out building was being held up by one rotten beam. He quickly tied one end of the rope to the back of the cart and then made a lariat with the other. Then, after spinning the lariat above his head, he lassoed the beam.

(Melrose and Brown 1998b: 10)

Here we can see that the subjectivity of both Zak and Justin is explored: '"You mean the place we nearly fried in," replied Zak, *recalling the time*'; and 'Justin *looked over his shoulder, anxiously*'. It is very slim but with an omniscient view we can see both Zak's and Justin's internal thoughts being revealed here through the inflection of 'recalling' and 'anxiously'.

The trick is to use it sparingly and give plenty of clues as to who is doing the thinking and talking by using 'he thought', 'she said', and so on, although this can be done subtly. For example:

She was angrier than she had ever been and wanted to tell them so. 'Just shut up, will you!'

'Oh come on, Josie,' sighed Amina. She could tell Josie was upset but wasn't sure why she had overreacted.

'Yeah, mate. Just cool it!'

'Leave it, Rachel,' added Amina. 'You're only making things worse.'

As if, thought Rachel. But she didn't say anything.

Yeah, thought Josie. Shutting up would be the best thing all round.

We will look at this in greater detail when we discuss dialogue, but here we can see a subjective glimpse of three characters who are identified for us by Amina as she comes between the two girls. We see how the subjectivity of Josie and Amina is dealt with directly but the sentence 'As if, thought Rachel' reveals a third perspective. This is much easier to execute when the three characters are members of a gang, or when they are in the same place, where the gang becomes the singular, with multiple voices. The classic example is Enid Blyton's Secret Seven. The golden rule is to keep the changes simple, make sure they interconnect and make sure everyone knows who is talking and why. (Certainly, this advice changes when we come to consider fiction for older readers, but it should be remembered that most adult fiction has only a limited number of subjective voices itself.) But you must never make this mixing and matching gratuitous chitchat that goes nowhere.

A familiar, restrained version of the unlimited can be seen in the first fifty pages of J.K. Rowling's *Harry Potter and the Philosopher's Stone*. In those early pages we receive subjective narrative from the Dursleys, Harry, Professor McGonagall and Dumbledore, although the text then turns to a more limited viewpoint as it proceeds. Crucially, in those first fifty pages, though, Joanne Rowling sets up the whole series without seriously deviating from the story's progress, and the subjectivity of the characters does not get in the way of the story about to unfold. Each character takes the story forward.

Another way to tackle multiple viewpoints is to separate them into chapters. Say you are writing about a couple of characters (perhaps they are writing to each other), you can allocate each their own space so it does not become confusing; a very good example of this is *Letters from the Inside* by John Marsden. A diary also allows you to introduce both third- and first-person narratives. Another excellent way is revealed in Melvyn Burgess's *Junk*, where he tells the story through four or five separate characters, but by this stage you are getting into the teen fiction market and the world of the more sophisticated reader.

THIRD PERSON LIMITED

This is a very effectual approach and probably the simplest and best approach when writing for children (especially in the earlier years). In its most extreme form, to write from a limited third person is to write entirely through the viewpoint of a single person without having to internalise the narrative (see 'First person', above). The benefit is to make an intimate association with the person whose view we are seeing. Check out books by Anne Fine, Jacqueline Wilson and Phillip Pullman, for example.

Children especially like this approach because initially, as they develop their storytelling skills, they write in the first person but like to read about others. This limited narrative is a good introduction to other storytelling techniques and to a point of view other than their own first person. Further, this very limited technique also allows them to empathise completely with the character you have created for them (presuming, of course, the character deserves empathy).

Let's look at Josie and Joe again:

> The moon sat high in the midnight-blue sky. Josie was amazed at how bright it was. She was watching a mouse snuffling around on the patio when suddenly it ducked out of sight. Josie looked around in case a cat was on the prowl. That was the moment when she spotted him leaning against the pergola. Her heart jumped. It was two in the morning and, like her, Joe shouldn't have been up. But there he was.
>
> It was a warm, muggy night. Probably can't sleep for the same reason as me, she thought. Josie watched him light a cigarette. 'I wonder what he's thinking,' she said softly to herself.
>
> Even though Josie had known Joe all her life, she hardly knew him at all. That didn't matter, though. Just as long as she could be close to him. That's what she really wanted.
>
> She watched him blow smoke up at the moon. It made her smile. Everything Joe did made her smile.
>
> The smoke curled like blue silk streamers in the moonlight. Now she knew. She was right to have sent him the letter. Seeing him standing there had convinced her. He would be thinking about her. She was sure of that.
>
> As he stubbed out the cigarette and turned to go back inside, Josie ducked behind the curtain. 'Goodnight, sweet Joe,' she whispered. She was hoping he would look up but was glad he didn't spot her.

A couple of cats snarled at each other. The still silence was broken. In her bed, Josie thought about nothing except Joe. Everything was going to be great.

What we can see is the scene being played out through Josie. It can be restrictive in that Josie always has to be in view, as it were, but unless you are writing for older age groups, starting at about age eleven or so, the limited point of view is almost a necessity. But do it well and it will be worthwhile.

In trying to explain this technique to my students I once referred to it as a 'camera following behind' approach. Later in classes, though, the students refined this when they referred to a whisper away from first person. Although it is essentially a third person omniscient, it allows a subjective, first-person viewpoint without the need to refer to the first-person pronouns.

Nevertheless, as Carol Saboda, one of my students, revealed in her Master's dissertation,[15] this can be refined even further to excellent effect. She took her third-person voice so close to her main character that it almost felt like we were reading the world through his eyes.

At first Carol was writing her piece conventionally:

Oddly enough, Jeremy did not mind the silence. If anything it was a relief, especially right after the accident. Most of all it distracted Them – his mother, his father, even his doctors.

The reference to 'Jeremy' and 'his' immediately reveals an omniscient voice. During discussion, though, Carol's fellow-students felt the use of 'his' to prefix 'mother' and 'father' was an encumbrance because the narrative voice was so close to first person anyway. So she changed the text to:

Oddly enough, he didn't mind it. The silence. If anything it was a relief, especially right after the accident. Most of all it distracted Them – Mom, Dad, even the doctors.

It could be argued that this is mixing third- and first-person viewpoint, but Carol went on to call it 'virtual first person' and used properly it can be very persuasive indeed. For another example you might like to read *Holes* (1999) by Louis Sachar. It is no more than a variant on the omniscient technique, but the intimacy is implicit and immediate. It takes us much closer to the main character without having to rely on the restrictive and often self-important inflection of *me, myself, I* when using the first person.

Hopefully, then, you have managed to make some sense of viewpoint. Once again, research it and practise it. It is the only way to get it right. Also try your first page in different styles: it is amazing how a small change from, say, third person limited to first person helps the story along (and vice versa, of course). But make sure you don't deviate. Mixing and matching may be interesting in certain experimental novels, but this will generally not do for a child reader. Don't jump between first person and third – at least not until you are writing for the more mature reader. Think about what is required. Think about what you like to read and why you like the viewpoint used. Even in this book the viewpoint I am using has to be consistent. I can't suddenly change; it is just not done . . . Well, actually, Andrew's viewpoint can and just did change. Were he to realise it, he has now shifted perspective from a first and second to a third person limited; then again it might be an objective, second person. Had he realised he might have apologised, but of course he is not as smart as he thinks he is. Who am I to be telling you this, though? Well you might ask! Speaking in the first person I am a little confused myself. One minute I had no voice and then I found myself the unknown narrator addressing you, the unknown reader. If it helps, I am younger than Andrew, certainly more handsome and you can call me on Brighton two, four . . . Oh! Here he comes . . . I'll catch you later.

The point is clear: choose your viewpoint carefully, then make it strong and interesting.

Whichever viewpoint you choose, however, the introduction of a third person into the proceedings gives you the opportunity to introduce change, not to the viewpoint (necessarily) but to the plot, character opinion and the course to be taken next as the story moves forward, which, as you know, it must do.

Pyramid plot structure

Beginning the beginning

I am often asked about how I plan a book. And the honest answer is that it varies. Sometimes I get an idea that takes months to germinate and then comes out in one giant writing burst. And, like Philip Pullman, sometimes I don't do revisions either. I just write lots of versions of the same book until I am satisfied with it. Other times, though, I organise the whole story, chapter by chapter, so I know what I am doing and where I am going next, revising as I go. My current novel (and therefore my best yet, I hope) has taken me over a year to write so far and I am only halfway through. I need a writing plan for this; otherwise I would forget all the good things I want to include. And writing books like this one, in between, or as well as, doesn't help me to finish the other. You might find this hard to believe, but as I write this book and my new novel, I have nine other books and some film scripts going through rewrites, editorial and other processes. For me and you, one simple piece of advice should always be followed: *keep a good notebook handy at all times!*

For the emerging writer, I recommend a writing plan. There are a number of reasons for this, but primarily it allows you to organise all the notes, scraps and ideas you gather in your notebook. A glance at my book reveals such a variety of ideas that you might wonder how I manage to write anything at all. This week I gathered quotations and snippets from Bruno Bettelheim, Jacques Derrida, Bob Dylan, Michel Houellebecq, Carl Jung and Charles Darwin. Ideas and connections are only useful to a writer when they can be linked into a useful, readable narrative, but I find that collecting ideas is a good catalyst for my writing.

I digress, though. It's a writer's lot and if you have read this you have indulged me – I crave order.

Since most writers who are just starting off write while they have jobs and other major distractions, I find setting up a plan helps a writer to know exactly what they are about to write as soon as they sit down. This seems a good idea to me: it saves time, heartache and those wasted, angst-filled hours of so-called writer's block (which I don't believe in).

If you block it is because you simply *don't know* what you should be writing next. But I digress again. Perhaps I should look at my own plan. Here it goes.

I try to set time aside, but life and jobs take over. As an academic, I have to keep odd hours. The important thing is to know what you are going to write when you sit down. That way the time you write doesn't really matter. *It's what you write that counts*. Planning, then, is all about moving your story forward. And all stories have to move forward, not just as a word count but as story progression. Sometimes it is useful to observe the growing stages. Indeed, I often see writing as *growing* a book. So let's move on past this seedling stage.

The etymological root of *plot* is *secret plan* and I rather like this description of it. It is the secret plan of the narrative you are about to present to your reader. This comes out in true linear form when presented as a novel, for example. But we all know how multi-layered, multi-accentual and dialogic[16] a novel is. Thus, the title 'pyramid plot structure' came by accident when I was trying to explain the beginning, middle and end alongside subplot, premise and the cause and effect of inciting incident. I realised that as I juggled all the balls in the air I could see what I was trying to do and say but there were too many voices all speaking at the same time. So I began ordering them into main plot, subplot, premise, beginning, middle and ends, and so on.

Before I go on with this, though, the first thing you have to look at is theme or subject matter. What are you going to write about? Why are you writing this story? But bear in mind there has to be something big at stake. Here are some familiar themes:

- Love
- Jealousy
- Hate
- Revenge
- Rivalry
- Maturity
- Power

When you tackle these, you have to ensure you write the *cause and effect* and the *action and reaction* to anything that takes place. If there is none, why did you write that chapter in the first place? Adding to this, we can look at basic plot ideas, such as:

- Questing
- Adventures
- Chase and pursuit
- Escape
- Rescue
- Temptation
- Transformation
- Maturation
- Love
- Forbidden love
- Sacrifice
- Metamorphosis
- Revenge

However, when constructing your plot the dictum *a good beginning, middle and end* is your biggest challenge.

In the section on 'story' (above) we looked at this constructively, and you cannot dismiss it now that you are thinking about putting your story down on paper. So let's look at it again briefly.

- *Beginning* Introduce the problem.
- *Middle* Develop the problem.
- *End* Solve the problem.
- *Outcome* Allow space for the reward.

And never underestimate the last of these. It's the dividend, the pay-off, the reward for finishing the novel, solving the crime and making sure your main character and reader have learned a very valuable lesson through the experience of the story – not as a didactic moral tale or happy-ever-after sweetening pill, but as an experience.

Planning the plot

There are a number of ways of doing this. My version is only a simple diametric example which you might find useful. Nevertheless it seems to work and while my students tease me endlessly about it, I see them using it time and time again without complaint. They often refer to it in their Master's theses. Let me show you the basic pyramid for a nine-chapter, 6,000–10,000-word story.

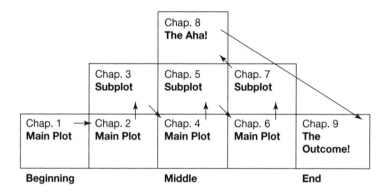

Try to follow the numbers. The 'aha' may look a little out of place perched on top there but that is because it is the king of the castle, the big issue; everything else has been setting it up, hence its positioning. In a linear fashion the same model would look like this:

Beginning

- Chapter 1 Main Plot Introduce the main hook, characters and problem.
- Chapter 2 Main Plot Develop the characters, hook, plot and dilemma.
- Chapter 3 Subplot Introduce distraction, partial/early achievement.

INTRODUCE THE INCITING INCIDENT

Middle (cause and effect/action and reaction)

- Chapter 4 Main Plot   Return to problem and develop it so that it worsens.

- Chapter 5 Subplot   Engage with the main plot in the problem development.

- Chapter 6 Main Plot   The problem/crisis is reaching its peak.

- Chapter 7 Subplot/   Intertwine as the crisis peaks.
             Main Plot

INTRODUCE THE CLOSING INCIDENT

End

- Chapter 8 The aha!   The problem/crisis is concluded/ solved.

DRAW TO A CLOSE

- Chapter 9 The outcome!   The end of the book.

As you can see, this system could be reduced for a smaller book and increased for a larger one, including a longer main plot and more than one subplot. Knowing roughly what each box will contain by writing a short thumbnail sketch or outline allows you to plan the story in advance.

Let's go forward, then, to look at each of these plotted stages in a little more depth.

Beginning

If you are thinking about easing your way into a child's book, think again. As Madonna is reported to have said to the President of Argentina when looking for permission to shoot the balcony scene in the film *Evita*, 'cut to the chase'. A little crude, perhaps, but it is better to think about diving straight in to start swimming immediately than floundering around while the story begins to take shape. Imagine if the short novel I have structured above were to begin like this (we'll stick with Josie and Joe in *Shooting Joe*):

> Josie yawned then stretched out on the lilo. She was enjoying herself very much. As the hazy sun gently warmed her face and the water rippled all around her, Josie sighed. She loved days like this. Long, listless days, just lazing around in the pool with no worries and no cares. When she looked over the garden, she could see Joe pointing the camera at her. She was right to have worn her new bikini. Everything was going swimmingly. She sighed again then pouted, as she stroked her hand through the water. Yes, she thought, everything was just perfect.

Where is this beginning going? It has said nothing of consequence yet. Indeed, we might suppose that Josie has nothing to do but lead the life of indolence. There certainly doesn't seem to be any incentive for a reader to keep reading, unless of course one finds indolence and watching paint dry interesting. But it depends on what we are expecting. If this were called *Sandy Cove* would we even want to read on? It is as boring as it sounds! What we are waiting for is the *event* to take place. Though if this novel was called *Shark Attack* we might be right in thinking a change is imminent, even if (post-*Jaws*) it's a little predictable.

Clearly, though, a change has to take place . . . and soon. Let's try *Shooting Joe* version two on a different tack:

> Josie wasn't a very good swimmer but at least she looked good lying on the lilo. She had worn her new bikini especially and it seemed to be working. As Joe fussed with the camera she was enjoying herself so much she hadn't seen Mary sneaking into the garden.
>
> In fact, Josie wasn't even aware Mary was there until Joe called out. 'Mary,' he shouted.
>
> Josie watched him put down the camera and run over to her. But as she leaned over, the lilo slid from under her.

Suddenly Josie was in the water. She swallowed some and coughed. She was feeling very silly. But when the cramp clamped her leg like a vice she knew she was in trouble. She grabbed at her leg and tried to keep afloat at the same time. Then she tried to grab the side. But she couldn't reach it. She was at the deep end and the bottom seemed a long way off as she sank below the water. The pain was excruciating. She was still sinking. There was nothing she could do. In her head she screamed for Joe but her mouth said nothing.

'Josie,' screamed Joe, at last. 'Josie!'

But Josie couldn't hear him.

OK, so it's a little melodramatic but at least it grips us immediately. The point is that the beginning is the only chance you have to get your reader to read on. Blow the beginning and you blow the book. My friend, the Oscar-nominated film director Jimmy Murakami, once told me the beginning in a television film has one job: to stop the viewer from going to the fridge or reaching for the remote. The beginning of a book is the same. Don't turn your readers off before you have a chance to turn them on. My own favourite beginning of all time is Charles Dickens's *Great Expectations*. Led with Pip down a gentle churchyard (with expectation), we get a short, sharp shock when Pip hears the words 'Keep still you little devil, or I'll cut your throat!' We have no choice but to read on.

When I began writing this book, I asked my daughter, aged seven, if she would write me the beginning of a story. Here is what she wrote: 'In the middle of the night Molly woke up. She had heard something . . .' As you can see, the story opens straight into the crisis. There is no point in hanging around for nothing to happen.

We can see this everywhere: from Dickens we saw the introduction of the problem was swift and immediate, even if it is a long time before we meet Abel Magwitch again. Indeed, I have often entertained the notion that edited Dickens for younger children would make excellent reading, except that he is probably worth waiting for.

The main tasks of the opening couple of chapters are:

- Introduce the theme.
- Introduce the main character.

- Introduce the setting.
- Introduce the premise.

It probably seems obvious even to the novice to say that these issues will be developed throughout, but you will be surprised at how often problems arise. I recently read a reportedly academic non-fiction book which was promoting the idea that none of us should be afraid of scholarship and research. But the author went on to blow the whole premise in the concluding chapters by criticising and writing off a *forthcoming* project before even reading it. The premise of 'scholarship and research' was ruined by a hypothesis based on ignorance, which of course can be the subject of research and scholarship but not the basis of it. Thus, the book is flawed by a paradox of its own making. And while there is some humour in contradiction, it is equally worrying. Surely no one would set out to write a contradiction unless it was meant to be funny or material to a plot, even in a provocative way, which begs the question: was the writer in control of the contradiction in the first place? If this seems extraordinary, however, be warned: all writers are capable of it. Be careful of projecting thoughts and ideas that cannot be substantiated.

Be careful, too, of letting the emotional self overtake the craft. The two have to go hand in hand. This plot structure, if nothing else, at least allows you to see where you are going next and where you have already been. Even a child will spot a contradiction a mile off.

So it is also crucial to remember that when you set up your premise it is like a horse: it's a bumpy ride but it can take you through the whole story. Continuing the metaphor, the old cliché 'you should never change horses in midstream' holds true, and yet I see this happening, too. It takes concentration to keep the narrative going forward.

Fix your premise in your head and ride with it, but make sure it doesn't trip itself up. Also, beware of being too didactic. You might find your religion, politics, sense of moral right and wrong, theories and ideas are a turn-off, downright offensive, possibly even wrong and can be proved to be so. You must consider this. And extending this point, personally I have no fear of censorship. It's the censors who worry me.

Middle

Moving on from the beginning of the book, you are entering the hardest part of the writing process. Once you have captured your reader's interest, you have to keep it. There is only one way to do this: *you must maintain the momentum of the story*. It must continue to go forward. And it does this by relying on conflict, crisis and change.

When I was discussing 'story' (above), I said the purpose of the middle of your story is to focus on the problem, which worsens through the inciting incident, and to introduce a focus of resistance such as suspense/surprise/tension, while your character changes and adapts to change, crisis and conflict. Let's look at the average plot chart again.

- The opening
- The arrival of conflict
- The early achievement
- The twist and change
- The denouement
- The final outcome

We have dealt with the opening and the arrival of conflict in the first couple of chapters. Now we need to think about developing the story.

When Aristotle said that the length of a drama should be such that the hero moves through a series of probable or necessary stages from misfortune to happiness, or from happiness to misfortune (although this latter is rare in children's writing and return to happiness is usually expected, especially for the young), it is wrong to think, now that the main characters, the opening and the conflict have been set up, that the rest of the novel is about constantly battling with the conflict. The average novel is much more than that. It is about development of the main character; it's about the emotional and physical survival of the main character in the conflict; and this development cannot take place in a vacuum, which is why we also develop a subplot and secondary characters who can assist in this development.

Subplot is very important. It could even be said that the subplot makes the rest of the story interesting, gives the story soul and can often be the real story, whereas the main plot just allows it to be told.

Therefore, it is important not to subvert the subplot as a minor plot. If all it does is contribute to the word count, then it shouldn't be there.

Even if you use the pyramid plot structure only as a diametric step outline, you should plan the incidents of your story to create situations in which your character develops. He or she must change through the various stages of conflict which you, the writer, inflict. Each experience comes to supplement those that went before. So your characters are seen to be accumulating experience as they proceed, to the extent that your novel comes to present a microcosm of the experience of life. Even if you are writing fantasy, the 'growth' of your central character is the same. At the same time, don't feel restricted by your step outline. It's only a guideline; if you feel your writing is pulling in another direction, then you can go with it, changing your step outline in sync with the changes. However, my strong advice here is *never* slip out of the story then back into it again just because you thought the distraction was interesting. You must consider whether it is doing any more than just boosting the word count. Cut the scene then read the novel again. You will invariably find you didn't need it in the first place.

Let's think about *Shooting Joe*. The beginning is easy and we have essentially dealt with that. We have an immediate crisis but it is multi-accentual. Think about this: Josie is in trouble in the swimming pool, but so, too, is her plan in trouble now that Mary has arrived.

In Chapter 2 of our pyramid plot we should be looking to develop Josie's plight. Perhaps we could go down the deaf-story route I introduced earlier.

> Josie stared at the doctor. He was opening and closing his mouth like a fish. It made him look stupid and she should have laughed. Except it wasn't funny. She didn't want to be here, surrounded by tubes and machines that blinked at her.
>
> He shone a light into her eye and that made her head hurt. Then he opened and shut his mouth again.
>
> She couldn't hear him saying, 'Josie, can you hear me?'
>
> She couldn't hear anything except her own thoughts.
>
> The words 'hello, teenager' echoed round and round in her brain. It was the last thing she remembered hearing. That was two days ago. Joe will never want her now!

Taking it for granted that Joe fished Josie out of the pool, although I would have written this, especially lingering on the kiss of life, we can see where the story goes next. Joe has managed to revive her, calling her 'teenager' when she wakens, and we can surmise Josie is in hospital. This has put the main plot and Josie's quest to seduce Joe at risk. Even when he comes to visit her in hospital it will be as a benign uncle/rescuer/hero-type figure (certainly in her dad's eyes – who, we will remember, loves his Jojo), which introduces the subplot.

This accident is undoubtedly a *crisis* as well as an inciting incident with a radical cause and effect, which is a setback for Josie, and indeed a setback for the main plot. As the main plot stumbles, we can see the subplot coming into view. Josie is taken home but life will have to change to accommodate her deafness. Thus, the subplot becomes this other struggle, while she tries to maintain her love interest in Joe. Of course, the issue of her having a pierced belly button has rescinded. Life has already taken a new and cruel twist. Meanwhile, Joe and Mary still have much to discuss. How will this setback impact on Josie? Has she got any motivation to recover? Does she want to hear what is in store for her? Is life going to be worth living for the new Josie? We can begin to see that perhaps there might be a story breaking here after all.

Trying to sort these sections out on your pyramid plot grid, they would look something like this:

	Chap. 3 **Subplot** In hospital Josie realises she has gone deaf. Life is coming to an end. How can she be happy now?
Chap. 1 **Main plot** Josie is making tentative friends with Joe and she gets into his film when he decides to film her in the pool.	Chap. 2 **Main plot** Mary arrives and, unbeknown to Joe, Josie gets into difficulty in the pool. Joe rescues her.

It is to be hoped you can see this making sense. What you need to pay attention to is the way the story progresses. Although it is worth saying here that each chapter provides a story of its own, and this is desirable, too. Thinking about each chapter as a single story helps that story to take on its own structure, with a beginning, middle and end. Consider this:

- Chapter 1
  - Beginning: Josie moves in on Joe
  - Middle: Joe offers Josie a part in his film
  - End: Josie is being filmed
- Chapter 2
  - Beginning: Josie is being filmed
  - Middle: Josie's life is a dream about to be shattered
  - End: Josie's in trouble
- Chapter 3
  - Beginning: Josie's in hospital – realises things are bad
  - Middle: Josie's sent home – things look no better
  - End: Josie's doting dad smothers her with love

Breaking down the chapters and story into components like this allows you to see what you have done in relation to what you are proposing to write next. And while it may look a little formulaic here, I can assure you it isn't. You still have to write the story. You still have to combine the creative with the craft, and this is where your creative skill comes into play – with play being the operative word. Remember what Freud said about play (see above). All you are doing here is ordering your playful creativity into a structure that a child reader can understand. And this is so important, too. While you may be able to follow the stream of consciousness in James Joyce's *Ulysses*, your average child reader (and your average adult reader, for that matter) craves order and structure. You only have to look at the way newspapers are 'ordered'. If this wasn't the case, the variations from paper to paper would be much greater than they are at present. After all, they are in competition with each other.

To conclude this section, then, the purpose of mapping out your story in the way that I have indicated merely allows you to chart the progress and development of your characters. The thumbnail sketches for each section can be as long or as short as you decide. Remember they are only guidelines, crib sheets, short memoranda for the piece that becomes your final story. The entanglements, wonder and advancement of your story ultimately rely on you. It is you and only you who can bring them all together because it is your story. It is you alone who can make it exciting, interesting and readable. But remember, you have to make it exciting, interesting and readable. Nothing else will do!

Also, try to remember how crucial the subplot is to the story. A subplot should never be gratuitous, but should reveal more about the development of the main character. It should also assist in moving the story forward. Make sure your subplot has its own structure, its own beginning, middle and end. If not, it is left dangling like a thread, which no tailor worth his salt would ever knowingly leave unfinished. Make sure you stitch it up before closing.

Having used Chapters 1 to 3 in your pyramid plot to set up your story, you are now in a good position to move on through the middle stage of the story. The developing plot structure would look something like this:

Chap. 5 **Subplot**	Chap. 7 **Subplot/Main Plot**
The doctors are mystified: there is no reason why she can't hear. Dad, Rachel and Amina try to cheer her up. But it's no use. She just wants to get back so she can see Joe again. Then she overhears Mary saying something. Yes, her hearing is coming back! But she doesn't want to admit it yet – she's getting fond of the attention.	Josie nearly lets the cat out of the bag about her hearing. It's a strain but she needs to spin it out until she discovers what Mary is up to. She spots Mary and Kazuo again. This time it's very confusing. As the subplot and main plot twist each other. Josie uses her (pretend) deafness to good effect.
Chap. 4 **Main Plot**	Chap. 6 **Main Plot**
Josie refuses to see Joe. She can't communicate and does not want his pity. On her way for a check-up she spots Mary with Kazuo. Meanwhile, Joe does come to see her and they have a laugh.	Josie decides to keep an eye on Mary and she is glad she does. Mary looks all too cosy with Kazuo and something is definitely up. Josie is concerned only for Joe's feelings. The daily laughs with Joe are great, though, and she is reluctant to tell everyone her hearing is back.

So the movement is a little more complex. In the subplot Dad, Amina, Rachel and Joe are all concerned about Josie's deafness. Josie, though, is enjoying the attention of Joe and thinks she has to fake her hearing problem in order for him to continue his visits. This leads her to see Mary's indiscretion. So, still feigning deafness, Josie tries to solve what is going on. *Or is it a red herring?*

As you can see from the above, I am leading Josie through a small mystery. I am dealing with the conflict and the crisis while Josie has to adapt and address change. What transpires in the 'aha!' moment, though, as we reach the end, is the most vital part of the book. Is it all too predictable, silly, unbelievable, or is there something deeper and more crucial about to be revealed?

As long as the story is leading you, maintaining your interest and keeping you reading, the only way to avoid the reader's ultimate disappointment is a good end. They deserve a good ending, one they didn't expect, a good twist, a shocker, a breathtaking ending of surprising simplicity but magical effect. Writing 'The End' is not enough. It never has been, and while the cliché 'they lived happily ever after' at least has a resonance of a continuing story, is *Jane Eyre*'s ending, 'Reader, I married him,' at all satisfactory? Don't we feel sorry for Jane with this forced ending?

Let's look at this, because ultimately the end of the book is the most important part.

End

Beginning the end is in some respects the story itself. Everything else has just been the preamble, the foreplay, the prolegomenon, the set-up. But the big question is: are you now ready to write the end? Do you really know what the end is? Are you sure you want to end here and now? I know some novelists who write the end first, or know the end before they know how they are going to tell the story. Jokes can be like that. If you know the punchline, you can tell the story any way you like because it is the punchline that counts. The same goes for a story, whether a novel, film or whatever: the end has to justify the means. Yet there are few of us so brave these days as to take up Charles Dickens's job. When he was writing *Great Expectations*, the early chapters were already being published in serial form before the novel was completed. Now that is what I call writing to a deadline. Of course, that's another issue. Why should the ending be attached to a deadline? It is the moment when the characters are screaming and kicking under the pressure of the narrative reaching the climactic crescendo. It is the live point when the central conflict is resolved once and for all. This is something to consider. How should you take the end screaming and kicking all the way to its climactic conclusion?

When you are thinking about how your story is going to end, you need to consider the premise of the story once more. What is the story about to convey? What message is being delivered? There seems to be little point in concluding in a way that contradicts your premise. Is there a message in the story you want to convey? If so, tell it simply.

THE AHA!

Taking a story to the end means reaching the moment of 'aha!', the point when all the elements of the story start to come together and make sense, the point when the reader can see the end in sight. In a curious oxymoron Aristotle said the ending should be both 'inevitable and unexpected'. How can it be both? The answer is simple. The inevitable – the shy guy finds his voice, the big-head gets her come-uppance, the stranger turns out to be known after all, the ghost is no ghost (or is it?) – of course was going to happen as the novel climaxed, but the way it happens has to be unexpected. In my book with Judy Waite, *Foul Play*, the premise of the novel is bullying and a change of school dilemma. As expected, the bully is revealed to everyone, but in a way that brings in an element of surprise. The bully was suspected and then accused of trying to fix a football match so his team could win. He protested his innocence because he was a sportsman who played by the rules of the game. It is eventually revealed that the fixer was the bully's victim. He had tried to fix the match because he didn't want further bullying to go on. Thus, the bully was made to realise the wider impact of his actions, and while he may be a sportsman on the football field, his bullying was revealed as 'foul play'. What is required of the unexpected is setting up a possible outcome, then putting the predictable and inevitable in doubt, suspending the inevitability until you are ready to reveal it in your own way. An early example of this can be seen in the work of Agatha Christie. It is inevitable the murder will be solved, but the surprise is in who committed the crime.

Let's look at Josie and Joe again, and the last section of the pyramid plot structure.

Chap. 8	Chap. 9
The Aha!	**The Outcome!**
Josie has used her pretend deafness to get her into a PoMo (position of maximum opportunity). But does she really hear what she thinks? Is there something else going on? The set-up takes us to the brink then pushes us over.	Josie feels like the kid she is and can't bring herself even to dislike Mary. She can see how good she is for Joe. She also feels a bit of a prat. Mind you, she thinks that Kazuo looks a bit of all right. All's well that ends well.

What is going on here? Josie enters the climax of the story through subterfuge, faking her deafness so that her rival, Mary, can be indiscreet in front of her (OK, so it's a little creaky – it's only an example). Let's try it.

> Josie spotted them by the park gate. She was trying to keep out of the way but it wasn't as easy as it looked. Hiding behind the lamp-post just made her look suspicious. As she got close to them she could hear them talking. She saw Mary smile as she took Kazuo's arm. 'Look, it's the kid who keeps mooching around Joe. Poor kid.'
>
> 'Shh! She'll hear us!'
>
> 'Don't be silly,' said Mary, 'she's deaf. Joe's just taking pity on her.'
>
> 'Well, even so. I don't want it getting out before we're ready.' Kazuo looked agitated. 'And he can't see me here. Not yet. After he has finished the film, like we agreed.'
>
> 'I know, but I can't wait to tell him, can you?' Mary smiled at Kazuo again.
>
> The two-timing rat, thought Josie. Then she wondered how she was going to tell Joe that his girlfriend was cheating on him.

Here we have the set-up. Josie has her evidence: Mary is two-timing Joe (how could she?). The inevitable is about to happen. Josie will tell Joe;

she has to. Her own chances rely on Joe finding out. It's perfect. Sad for Joe, of course, but he'll get over it when Josie steps into Mary's shoes.

So how does it pan out?

'Must have been a virus,' said the doctor. 'Whatever it was, though, it's cured now. Josie's hearing is perfect.' The doctor unplugged the hearing-test machine and put it away.

'Thank goodness for that, Jojo!' said Dad.

Josie didn't mind being called Jojo. She was just pleased everyone was so happy with her progress. Even Joe had hugged her. It had been a strain keeping up the pretence, but she had managed to get away with it. The only problem now was how she was going to tell Joe about Mary . . .

Later that night Josie finally got a chance to speak to Joe alone. 'Joe, yesterday, when I thought my hearing was coming back, I overheard Mary talking to someone.'

'Oh yeah, who?'

Josie fidgeted. 'It was another boy.'

Joe smiled at her. 'A boy, eh? Well I'd better watch out, hadn't I?'

Josie grinned uncomfortably back at him. Just then Mary came into the room.

'What's this about you and some other bloke. Seeing him behind my back, are you?' Joe was half laughing at first. Then he saw Mary's reaction.

Gotcha, thought Josie, without saying it out loud.

'Mary? What's up?' asked Joe.

Get out of that, thought Josie, still not saying anything.

Mary looked long and hard at Josie, then at Joe. 'I was going to tell you . . .'

'Tell me what?' asked Joe.

'That she's got another bloke!' spluttered Josie. 'She's a two-timing rat and she should have told you ages ago. He came down from Durham with her and they have been meeting on the sly!'

Joe looked stunned. 'Mary?'

So it's done. The dirty deed is finally out in the open. Josie is triumphant, Mary will be history and then the story really begins.

> Mary looked shocked and disturbed at the same time. 'It's not what you think.'
>
> 'I don't know what I think,' said Joe. 'I mean, what am I to think? What's going on, Mare?'
>
> Josie cringed at Joe's pet name for Mary.
>
> 'It was meant to be a surprise.' Mary sighed. 'Only we wanted to let you finish the film first. You were already distracted by the minx here,' Mary nodded in Josie's direction, 'and, well, we knew you had to finish the final scenes before the deadline.'
>
> Joe shrugged at her. 'We? Who's we?'
>
> 'Me and Kazuo!'
>
> Joe looked stunned again but then he broke out into a huge smile. 'Kazuo!' he shouted. 'You mean Kaz's here, in Brighton?'
>
> 'Yeah.'
>
> 'But that's brilliant, I thought he wasn't due back 'till next month.'
>
> Mary grinned. 'They wrapped up early and he flew back as soon as he could.'
>
> 'That is so brilliant.' Joe smiled. 'He can help me with the cut. Where is he? Oh Mary, you should have said.' Joe's smile was as bright as the moon.
>
> Josie's face was as bright as a tomato. She had no idea what was going on but her plan was clearly going wrong.
>
> Mary smiled back. 'He made me wait until you had time for him. You know what he's like: film first, everything else can wait.'
>
> 'Wait? I can't wait to see him. Come on,' said Joe, 'let's go and get him.' He looked over at Josie. 'See you later, minx.'
>
> Josie watched Joe and Mary turn to walk away. She felt a fool.
>
> But Joe looked back and winked at her. 'Kazuo's my all-time best friend. He's been working on a documentary in Alaska this past year. I haven't seen him in ages.'
>
> 'Oh!' said Josie as Joe and Mary closed the door behind them.

And as we close the door, we reveal the climax twisting the tale into a different conclusion from the predicted one. Or do we? Kazuo and Mary could still have been up to some jiggery-pokery. Closing the door like this, though, allows us to extend the agony until finally we can take everything to the resolution.

Of course, *Shooting Joe* may look completely different after I have finished it. After all, it's only a scrapbook of ideas I am toying with. Playing, as Freud would have it. Who can tell? But I have made it deliberately simple so that at least you can see a plot unfolding, through the beginning, middle and end. And the final outcome? Well, Josie feels a twit. She got it all wrong and her two and two made one fine mess. Joe forgave her, though, because she was only looking out for him. Mary thought it was a bit of a laugh: after all, Josie's just a kid. Mind you, Kazuo is good looking. Josie was already beginning to think he had potential . . . Will she ever learn?

One final word on this. The pyramid plot structure can be as high and wide as you like, but it is not a panacea. It is simply a working model. However, try experimenting with even the most basic story, or take someone else's story in an experiment. You will find, for example, even the picture book *Can't You Sleep Little Bear?* (Martin Waddell and Barbara Firth, 1988) fits into this model very well. Instead of chapters, think of it as developing story stages. And, of course, that picture book has quite a strong contrasting plot and subplot.

		Aha! 6 The answer		
	Subplot 2 Big Bear wants to read	**Subplot 4** Big Bear wants to read		
Main Plot 1 Little Bear can't sleep	**Main Plot 3** Little Bear can't sleep	**Main Plot 5** Little Bear can't sleep	**Finish 7** The **ah!** factor

Main plot: Little Bear can't sleep and it's too dark. Subplot: Big Bear wants to read his book. The end happens with both getting what they want. A simple plot with a big story which, with patience and care, could be extended into the biggest novel you have ever written.

Using the template below you can simply make something up yourself and fill in the blanks, showing chapter numbers. Then write thumbnail sketches of each chapter, working out what each one is going to say before making a start. This is for twenty chapters, scenes, but, of course, this can be enlarged or reduced as necessary. Remember, this is not *gospel*; it is a template to enable you to see what you are writing. I can assure you I have seen this work time and time again.

			Aha!			
			Inciting Incidents	Closing Incidents		
		Minor Plot				
	Subplot					
Main Plot						Closure

The inciting and closing incidents can come in when you choose (see the plan in 'Story', above), although the inciting incident usually comes in fairly quickly and the closing incident precedes the 'aha' moment, which draws the whole story together. They sit at the top of the structure to emphasise their importance, along with the 'aha' moment, which leads to closure, not because they are in the middle of the story. The closing incident and 'aha' moment are usually at the conclusion of the story.

This is a loose plan. The issues will intertwine, cross over and collide with each other as you write. But you can see the separations and how the story can conceivably be constructed in a useful way. It allows you to see the story growing and to see how your story can be paced. As Robert McKee has written, structure is a collected selection of events from the characters' life stories that are brought together into an integral sequence to arouse specific emotions and express the specific view of life the writer wishes to reveal. Using this diametric model, you can collect the appropriate events as chapters to construct the story you wish to tell. For example:

- *Main Plot* This is the main part of the story. It is where your character comes from and is going to. In *Shooting Joe*, for example, it is Josie's pursuit of Joe.

- *Subplot* This can be something else that is going on in the life of the characters. In *Shooting Joe* it could be the film they are making, along with Josie's battle with her dad and her deafness, if we keep it. Essentially it is what supplements and also gets in the way of the main plot (life gets in the way).

- *Minor Plot* Both Josie and Joe have turmoil in their lives. Josie's mother is gone (dead?), her father is not coping and so on. Joe, meanwhile, is concerned about Mary.

Adding the inciting and closing incidents, the 'aha' factor and the final closure, we have a good structure in which to tell the story of *Shooting Joe*.

But don't take my word for all of this. Try your own story.

Of course, in the plot construction you will also be investing all the emotions, events, conflicts, activities, jokes, scrapes, dreams, quests, moods, images, witty *bons mots*, gritty dialogue and personalities which make up your story. Further, if a particular section does not work as it should, like a dodgy brick in a wall it can simply be pulled out and replaced. Philip Pullman, for example, comes up with his plots by writing short scenes on tiny yellow Post-it stickers and puts them all on a big sheet of paper.[17] He can then juggle them around to see how best the story goes and then he can write them up one by one. This is just a variation on the theme I have already outlined. Do whatever works for you. I am about to try Post-it stickers on a pyramid plot structure for my next novel. I can just stick them on and tear them off as I see fit.

Dialogue

Dialogue is crucial to children's fiction. A recent request from a publisher who wants me to write for her contained the following caveat: 'Dialogue is very important!'

You would think it would be easy to write it. After all, virtually all of us can speak. So why is dialogue often the main thing that lets down good writing? Perhaps it is because most fledgling writers do not pay attention to the simple fact that written dialogue is not the chatter of everyday life. Let's face it, everyday life is generally pretty dull.

> 'Terrible weather.'
> 'Isn't it!'
> 'Feels like it's been raining for ever.'
> 'Feels like I've been waiting on this bus for ever.'
> 'It's getting worse.'
> 'I know. I waited twenty minutes yesterday.'
> 'The rain, I mean.'
> 'I blame the government.'
> 'Not much they can do about the weather.'
> 'No, but at least we used to be able to catch a bus when it rained.'

Okay, I nudged up that little routine into a little joke but I had to. Listening to the average conversation, you will realise that it's not worth repeating verbatim. Try taping a conversation to see for yourself. It's full of stumble, pauses, poorly chosen words, half words, repetition, odd phrasing, and, depending on the speakers, can often rely on 'prior knowledge'.

> 'So how are things in Echelfechin?'
> 'Fine, yer dad visited her yesterday.'
> 'He shouldn't be driving.'
> 'It wasn't too bad. The gritters had been out.'
> 'That's not what I meant . . .'
> 'Aye well, there's no telling him.'
> 'No! All the same . . .'
> 'He took an electric blanket. Just in case . . .'
> 'What about a food parcel?'

'She doesn't get much money from the social.'

'So you sent her some? She's perfectly capable of working, you know.'

'Hey, you'll never guess who I saw yesterday? D'you remember . . .'

'You're changing the subject.'

'Aye well . . .

As you can see from the above, the conversation will go on and on until you decide to stop. It avoids closure. It develops our intimacy and our ongoing relationship, but reveals very little about our relationship. Nor does it take the story forward, unless of course you were to know that I (as first-person narrator) am speaking to my (fictional) mother and the 'her' from Echelfechin is my (fictional) waste-of-space sister.

Unless you want to bore the child reader to death, start to consider what dialogue does for a story.

Dialogue is not straight conversation. It is a literary convention with a purpose all of its own. It is all about giving your characters charisma, charm, temperament, emotions, interesting ideas, life. If I was to take the Echelfechin story into proper literary account, for example, it would go something like this (and I'll leave you to guess the viewpoint in use).

Goodness, she must have been sitting right on the phone. 'Hi!'

'Oh, hiya! Everything all right?'

I should call more often if that's what she thinks every time I do call. 'Does anything have to be wrong for me to give my mother a call?'

'No, I just wondered, that's all.'

That's my mother. She spends her life wondering and worrying. And if she has nothing to worry about she wonders if she should have. 'I just thought I'd give you a call and see how things were in Echelfechin.'

'Och, you know how it is.'

I knew all right. My waste-of-space sister is playing up again and my folks are getting too old to keep bailing her out.

'Yer dad went up yesterday.'

'He shouldn't be driving.'

'It's OK. The gritters have been out.'

'That's not what I mean and you know it.' He was supposed to take life easy after his operation. Fat chance of that when Lady Muck wants a hand. 'So how is she, anyway? She knew when she married him he would have to work away. He can hardly clock on nine till five, can he? That's not the way lighthouses work.'

'Och, I know, but she gets lonely.'

'Never mind her, though. How are you? You coping OK.'

'Oh, me, I'm fine.'

Of course she's fine. She's always fine. Even when she had bowel cancer she was fine. As if she would say anything else! It's just not her way. 'I thought I might come up this weekend. If it wouldn't be any trouble, that is.'

'Trouble, how could you be trouble. It'll be great to see you. Will you fly up? Dad could pick you up at the airport . . .'

I was shaking my head. Luckily, she couldn't see me.

As you can see, I have set up the dialogue to give you a domestic background involving:

- a son who lives away
- a sister who can't accept her lot
- a father who should be taking it easy
- a brother-in-law who works away as a lighthouse keeper
- a mother who puts up with anything life gives her.

It is fairly commonplace stuff but at least the initial conversation has been fleshed out. All the ingredients are there, but it's still pretty boring. Let's face it, other people's domesticity isn't very interesting unless you are setting up something major. So we have to conclude that this kind of chitchat is gratuitous unless it leads to a significant revelation. Well, the planned trip to Scotland could be useful, but then it could have been revealed much more simply, with much of the domestic dialogue cut out:

As Colm walked to the terminal he dialled a number on his mobile and waited for it to ring. 'Hi. It's me!'

'Oh, hi. What's that noise? Where are you?'

'At the airport. The Edinburgh flight leaves in half an hour.'

'Are you coming home, then?'

'Thought I might. Get a chance to catch up.'

'That'll be nice. I'll get yer dad to pick you up.'

'No, he's not supposed to be driving. I'll take a taxi. See you in a couple of hours.'

'OK then.'

'Bye.' Without breaking stride, Colm pressed the disconnect button and shoved the phone into his coat pocket. He was looking forward to seeing his family again. Time he had a word with his sis, too.

Now it is all about a journey to somewhere 'other' without the formalities of going through the boring stuff. And yet we find out:

- Colm's at the airport
- he's going home
- his mother is happy about it
- his father shouldn't be driving
- he has something to say to his sister.

Even transition dialogue like this needs to be precise. And, as we can see, the story is moved on considerably even in this short piece.

In my experience children love reading dialogue. They love the way it breaks into the page of prose and into their heads as the spoken word. But you still need to cut out the mundane because in the main it is just plain dull. However, dull information can be crucial to the plot, so it has to be made more interesting. In *Shooting Joe*, let's consider a dialogue that might have taken place between Josie and her two friends, Amina and Rachel. A further point to consider here is how the introduction of a third person, rather than a plain two-way conversation, introduces potential conflict, humour, tension and any number of options because of the way it allows two characters to play off against the third. Of course, this can work from humour all the way through to tragedy. Romeo and Juliet, Othello and Desdemona *et al.* would have been fine without the third influence on their lives.

Josie looked blankly at Amina and Rachel. Pretending she couldn't hear was getting to be harder than she had imagined.

Amina pulled a face then said to Rachel, 'Isn't it funny how Josie has become more interesting now that she can't hear a word we say?'

'That's because we can say what we like in front of her,' replied Rachel. 'I mean, before she could get so crabby at the slightest tease.'

'What are you two saying?' asked Josie.

'Here, I'll write it down for you,' replied Rachel, which she realised was a waste of time. She wrote on Josie's pad: *I said it's no fun not being able to tell you jokes.*

Josie cast Rachel a frown as if to say, Yeah, right. But she didn't say it out loud.

Then Amina took the pencil and wrote: *I was just saying how much I missed you.*

Josie wanted to scream at them, but she knew it was best not to. She couldn't let her secret out. Not yet, anyway.

Amina giggled. 'Silly prat!' she said.

Rachel joined in. 'Silly's too good a word. But she is a prat if she thinks that Joe is going to fall for her.'

'He is a hunk, though,' added Amina. 'I mean, you have to admit that.'

Josie gave her a quizzical look.

Amina picked up the pad again and wrote: *We were just wondering if you will have to go to another school.*

'I wasn't born yesterday,' replied Josie. 'You must think I'm d . . . ' She almost let her secret out of the bag. 'You must think I'm blind. I saw your lips moving and you definitely said the word "prat"!'

Amina giggled and wrote: *No I didn't, I said "perhaps". You must have been mistaken.*

'Yeah, right,' conceded Josie. 'Look, I'm getting tired now, would you mind going?' She wasn't tired but the effort of pretending she was deaf was getting to be a bit of a strain. One more insult from Amina might be too much to bear. Besides, she wanted to check out Mary. There was definitely something fishy going on and Josie wanted to find out what it was.

'Come on, Rachel,' said Amina, 'let's leave the little prat to her silence.'

Rachel giggled, then smiled at Josie. 'See you, prat face!'

Josie smiled back and said, 'Bye!' Her secret was safe for now, but she was biting her lip. Just you two wait, she thought, as they left.

Having this conversation with Josie pretending not to be able to hear allows us to use a little irony while putting Josie on the spot and testing her resolve. Of course, it also serves to dish up some humour, lets us know how cruel kids can be and reveals a side to Amina and Rachel. In other words, it's character-building. But so, too, is the plot moving forward in this scene. Josie needs to get rid of them because she needs to keep her secret. Why? Because she wants to check out Mary, and being deaf will allow her to listen for indiscreet talk; on which, of course, the plot hinges. I have also left in the small subplot that she will get back at Amina and Rachel when the time comes (and so should make a note: 'Do not to forget to tie this loop at an appropriate time').

Important in this scene is the way in which Amina and Rachel exploit their dialogue/triangle to good effect. Introducing the third person into a conversation opens up the potential for change. Try this: have two people speaking, then introduce a knock at the door, a telephone ringing, something said on the radio, a kid brother bursting into the room, a mother interfering. This provides immediate change, and change is what is needed for the story to progress. The third voice also introduces empathy, sympathy, support, opposition, ganging up, ganging against, and so on. This is because a dialogue between two people is generally more intimate. A talks to B and B talks to A, back and forth. Introducing another voice, C doesn't just make a threesome but introduces the factor three to the equation to give six options. See the diagram opposite on page 69.

Thus, there is more potential to open out the dialogue and widen the subject matter, give facts and so on. However, once it goes beyond three people it starts to get tricky and crowded: the characters can't get a word in edgeways or one gets sidelined. While this can be used to good effect, generally it is best to work around three voices.

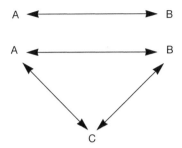

Something which must also be considered is the connection between dialogue and internal thoughts and subjectivity. Contradictions and paradoxes between external and internal issues can be addressed. Externally, Josie may be concerned about Joe (internally, too), but there is also the issue of her dead mother, which remains unspoken yet festers. Consequently, emotional and moral conflicts need to be resolved at the end of the story as part of the dramatic plot. Unless, of course, you are writing *King Lear* and Lear is slowly going mad (there's not much call for this, though). For example, if Josie's exterior dialogue and demeanour contradict her internal feelings, it is best to get them reconciled at some point before the story closes. The same goes for her relationship with her father.

You should also consider punctuation. There are no hard and fast rules (apart from the fact that every time you introduce a new speaker you *must* start a new paragraph), however, let me highlight some of the more obvious ones.

Generally, a comma precedes a sentence of dialogue if the speaker is introduced.

- Example 1 Amina giggled, then nodded at Josie, 'See you around . . .'

  The dialogue starts with a capital but it is not a new sentence as such because it carries the 'communication' information: the nod at Josie signifies the direction of the dialogue. It is being pointed at Josie. The other way is to open with dialogue and continue the sentence outside the parenthesis.

- Example 2 'See you around,' said Amina, nodding. Then she turned and walked . . .

Amina delivers a nonchalant, almost throwaway line here. Another example of this is to write a complete sentence in parentheses to alter the effect.

- Example 3 'You know, Josie. I really don't like you!' Amina turned to go.

Here we can see the way punctuation emphasises delivery: short, sharp and precise. Another way is to break up the sentence.

- Example 4 'You know, Josie,' said Amina, 'I really don't like you!'

The commas after 'Josie' and 'Amina' help to introduce a pause and sense of realism to the phrasing, but it is less emphatic and more defensive. In Example 3's 'don't like you' Amina sounds angry; in Example 4's she is more hurt or disappointed, resigned even. Another way to do this is to use full stops and question marks.

- Example 5 'I don't like you, Josie,' said Amina. 'I mean, why should I?'

- Example 6 'Why should I like you, Josie?' Amina was crying. 'Tell me why?'

The comma, full stop, question mark and exclamation mark, used judiciously, can turn the reading experience into one where the communication becomes more than the two-dimensional word on the page. A shrug accompanied by a tailing piece of dialogue can often say much more than a full explanation in a show-not-tell way.

Andrew shrugged at his editor. 'Think they'll get that, Anna?' Anna smiled back reassuringly at the author. Nothing more needed to be said.

Some important dialogue tips

- As you can see from the above examples, it is best not to be too explicit. The exchanges between Amina and Rachel give just enough of themselves without having to be explained in any detail. For example:

  > Amina giggled. 'Silly prat!' she said.
  >   Rachel joined in. 'Silly's too good a word. But she is a prat if she thinks that Joe is going to fall for her.'
  >   'He is a hunk, though,' added Amina. 'I mean, you have to admit that.'

- Keep the dialogue short and pithy. You are not writing Hamlet's soliloquy.

- Don't bury the important information in the middle of a speech. Either lead with it or close with it: 'He is a hunk, though,' added Amina.

- Keep it simple. Listen to children talking: they rarely hypothesise on the thermo-nuclear ramifications of big-bang theory when considering the theological implications of the creationists.

- Avoid repetition unless it is for effect, like humour (but make sure it is funny):

  > 'He is a hunk, though,' added Amina.
  > 'Yeah, he is a hunk,' replied Rachel.
  > 'Too right,' said Amina.
  > 'Yeah, too right,' said Rachel.

  What is funny about that? It's certainly repetitive.

- Avoid cliché (like the plague).
- Avoid ellipses . . .

  > 'You mean . . .'
  > 'Yeah, I mean . . .'

> 'Goodness, who would have thought, you know . . .'
> 'Well, it just goes to show.'
> 'Doesn't it just . . . I mean . . .'

Conversations are replete with pauses and anticipation but consider how much information you are getting over when doing this. It's OK now and then for effect . . . but don't litter the page with dots . . .

- Always start a new paragraph when changing speaker. It seems obvious, but you would be surprised how often it is missed in drafts.

- Does the dialogue sound right when read out loud? If not, it's not working.

- Do the speaking characters interact and still manage to push the story forward? They should!

- Be careful with slang, colloquialisms, jive talk, teen talk and profanities. Nothing dates dialogue more than this. Even when I was reading comics, 'cool, daddio' wasn't hip. Although 'cool' seems to be cool again now. With profanities, it is a question of age and a little thoughtfulness. Sometimes only 'Shit!' will do – if you have tried to say 'toffee' after hitting your thumb with a hammer you will know what I mean. But used sparingly it increases the effectiveness. Slang words are problematic, too. They can date a text terribly and colloquial speech has to be realistic: 'Know what I mean, guv, love a duck, down the apple and pairs in me old tin flute.' It's all a case of thinking about what you want to say and how to say it in the best way. It is best to get the flavour and texture of what you want to say without having to patronise or, worse still, getting it wrong.

- Avoid being patronising, my dear.

- Be careful with gender issues. Boys and girls are different, but don't go down the 'sugar and spice/slugs and snails' route.

- Be careful with age. Don't make the mistake of patronising your reader's intelligence. At nursery school once a parent picked up my son's toy, saying, 'Here's your little dinosaur.'

'It's not a dinosaur,' replied Daniel, 'it's a Euplacephalus.' He was three.

- Be careful, too, with race and class.

- Beware of bad regional dialects. Unless you are really sure, you should skip it. Remember Dick Van Dyke in *Mary Poppins*! It is better to get a slight nuance of place rather than bad delivery.

- Finally, silence can speak louder than words. As we can see from the example below, Josie's cursory 'Bye!' hardly accounts for the initial set-up. Nevertheless, it is very effective in setting up something that can be settled later.

> 'Come on, Rachel,' said Amina, 'let's leave the little prat to her silence.'
> Rachel giggled, then smiled at Josie. 'See you, prat face!'
> Josie smiled back and said, 'Bye!' Her secret was safe for now, but she was biting her lip. Just you two wait, she thought, as they left.

Dialogue doesn't have to be all 'she said', 'so I said', 'then he said', 'so we said' and so on. It can be refined and effective, but don't worry about using the word 'said'. It has become such a part of our reading process that we hardly notice it. But try to vary it a little: think about what you want to say, then think about how you would say it yourself.

It is easy to address a speaker through other means, and you shouldn't baulk it if it works. For example:

> 'Hi, Saidhu!'
> 'Hey, Danny, how are you?'
> Danny frowned. He would like to have said he was fine but that wouldn't have been true.
> 'You OK, Dan? You look kinda peaky.'
> 'Sure, Sai. Just got something on my mind, that's all.'
> Saidhu smiled then shrugged. 'Anything I can do to help, buddy?'

'Nothing can help him,' whispered Suzie, in Saidhu's ear. 'I'm the problem.'

I haven't used any 'he said' tags here until I identify Suzie (and the point of conflict), but it is pretty clear who is talking to whom. And that is the crucial issue. If there is any doubt about who is speaking then you are not doing your job (unless that is part of the plot). Of course, once again we can see how the triangle introduces the point of change.

'It's all about being clear,' he said.
Andrew said, 'It's all about being clear.'
'Be clear about it,' said Andrew.
'Is that clear?' Andrew asked.
'As mud,' replied Andrew.
'Are you talking to yourself again?' asked Anna.
'He always does that,' chipped in his children.
Anna shook her head. 'I'm glad I'm only his editor.'

Prose

I do not want to say too much about prose because it is such a subjective topic. But we might ask what is it? My dictionary defines prose as: 'spoken or written language as in ordinary usage distinguished from poetry by its lack of marked metrical structure'. I disagree. As W.H. Auden wrote, 'The difference between verse and prose is self-evident, but it is a sheer waste of time to look for a definition of the difference between poetry and prose' (Auden 1963: 23). I think David Lodge got it entirely right when he said, 'The golden rule of fictional prose is that there are no golden rules – except the ones that each writer sets for him or herself' (Lodge 1990: 94).

Italo Calvino referred to his own set of rules as 'exactitude'. He writes:

For the ancient Egyptians, exactitude was symbolised by a feather and served as a weight on scales used for the weighing of souls . . . To my mind [as a writer], exactitude means three things above all:

1. a well-defined and well-calculated plan for the work in question;

2. an evocation of clear, incisive, memorable visual images; in Italian we have an adjective that doesn't exist in English, 'icastico' . . .;

3. a language as precise as possible both in choice of words and in expression of the subtleties of thought and imagination.

(Calvino 1996: 55)

As you can see, Calvino's small set of exactitude rules bridges the gap between the setting of a plan and the execution of it, right down to his choice of words.

You will see differences in writing through the way nouns, pronouns, verbs, adverbs, adjectives, metaphors, metonyms, synecdoche and silence as hypothetical postulate work. Don't worry about these terms, you should have a very good dictionary (if not invest well because you surely need one) and you can look them up. But going back to prose, it is the richness of it that we can and must tailor to suit ourself, our story and our reader. Creative writing is all about mastering language and then using all the other skills to assist you in writing intentionally. Surely this is what Italo Calvino meant when he referred to exactitude. It cannot be just craft alone; it has to be 'a language as precise as possible both in choice of words and in expression' which combines with 'the subtleties of thought and imagination'. In short, craft alone will do nothing without critical creativity.

But looking again at language, Philip Pullman said that, for him, 'prose should be a plain glass window and not a fanciful mirror' (in Carter 1999: 184). There is something very persuasive about this. He is not trying to say it should be so plain and workmanlike to make it downright drab and see-through. What he is saying is it has to be transparent but there is also the surface of the glass to be seen. There are many ways to approach a window. While you still need to see through it to see where the story is going, you need not spend all your time peering through. You can allow your narrative to pause by the ledge occasionally or to check the reflection in the glass (and I hope I haven't been too metaphorical here). This idea allows for some reflection, which enriches the story without displaying the mirror-reflective narcissism of the writer, which can become intrusive. If we are vain enough to be writers in the first place, we do not need to spend our lives, Narcissus like, staring into mirrors. We should be projecting, not self-reflecting. For example:

> Prose is the very essence of your writing, it is the narrative from your heart, the window into your inner voice, the timbre of your very soul . . . *Goodness, what am I saying to these people. The more I write the less I seem to know. This book is only going to be any use if I know more than the reader, but do I? And what if I get them to look out of the window and they see nothing . . . I can't write this book . . . I don't have the skill . . .*

OK, that was just a tease (or a moment of self-doubt, which we all experience). I am not so racked with self-doubt now that I can't compose myself and settle down to it again. But too much reflection can make writing too difficult for a child reader to take forward. It has to be just right, but this doesn't mean we cannot let our characters have space to reflect on their own positions. Here is an example from Josie, again.

> As Josie lay in her hospital bed, great swathes of her recent past came hurtling back at her. Not the accident in the swimming pool. She remembered little about that. Perhaps time would help her to remember that. But what was troubling her most right now was her mother. Even after two years, Josie missed her mother more than anything in the world. Suddenly her silent sobbing came in great gulps, waking her up in the process. Now she was awake. After all this time, the long nights of loneliness were back. Only this time, apart from her own lonely thoughts, there was the silence, too. Even daybreak couldn't fix that.

We can take a moment to allow Josie's emotions to come to the fore. It does not have to be long pages of gut-wrenching heartache;

just enough reflection in the window before we look out again will do.

What I propose to do here is give a few other examples of what can be done with prose, from the very simple through to the more complex.

Example one

> Tom did not like the look of the man.
> 'Come on, Tom,' said Mum.
> Still Tom didn't budge. The man looked strange.

Here we are looking at an early read-to/read-alone piece of prose, for ages four to six. It is simple and straight to the point, with a crisis looming.

Taking it up a notch to ages six to eight, though, we can begin to introduce a simile and perhaps even a small metaphor.

Example two

> Tom did not like the look of the man. He thought he had strange eyes. They popped out of his head *like a frog's*.
> 'Come on, Tom,' said Mum.
> Still Tom didn't budge.
> The *frog-eyed man* stared at him.

The simile is easy to spot: '*like a frog's*'. But the small metaphor of the '*frog-eyed man*' works, too. Because we are linking the metaphor to the initial simile, we are not taxing the reading skills too much, and provided this isn't overused the reading becomes more of a pleasure. Of course, the metaphor has to stay simple. If I had written, 'the man's *Sprite eyes*', would anyone have known what the metaphor was? Back in the sixties and early seventies the Austin Healy Sprite sports car was nickname the Frog-eye. Setting your prose is all about trying to get the reading level right: being too smart can be just as bad as not being smart enough (and, be honest, would you have worked out the displacement of the Sprite to a frog-eye car as a metaphor for frog-eyed?). The secret here is not to get too smart for smart's sake. Make the metaphors and similes count. Writing is not all about what you know but what you can give.

Prose is all about clarity. And your story has to be clear, hence Philip Pullman's window metaphor. Nevertheless, pausing for a moment doesn't have to be just window-dressing. I particularly like the extended, epic or Homeric simile. This is where the ordinary simile is taken to greater depth of expression and expansion. It works for the older age group of eight to ten.

Example three

> Tom did not like the look of the man, who was staring oddly at him. He shuffled nervously.
>
> Suddenly the man's eyes began to bulge. They didn't look real. In fact Tom thought they were like two white mice with pink noses, nearly popping out of his head. Tom half expected to see a whole army of mice spewing out of his head any second now. But there was something else worrying him. In his head, Tom could hear a roar like thunder and flashes of electricity seemed to zip all around the room in front of his eyes. But worse than that, the whole world felt as though it was shaking beneath him.
>
> The man with the bulging eyes went on staring.
>
> 'Come on, Tom,' said Mum.
>
> Still Tom didn't budge. He shivered; the earthquake persisted. It was like the man was trying to see into the dark reaches of Tom's very soul and he couldn't keep him out.

OK, so this is not Homer (or Philip Pullman, for that matter, who writes wonderful epic similes in *His Dark Materials*), but we can see how the reading-age experience is being enhanced with a little attention to the prose. Extending the simile to thunder, lightning, earthquakes and dark reaches of the soul tugs at the extent of Tom's concern. The tension is heightened, the potential crisis is greater than it was considered earlier, yet the story is essentially the same. Try this out for yourself, and, if you want better examples, read *His Dark Materials* to see a master of his craft at work. It really is worth the effort and I take my hat off to Philip Pullman for it (funny how my use of cliché works so well here: sometimes it says all that is needed).

Example four

Going back to Italo Calvino, one of the enduring aspects of his work is the way in which he writes a detail, then subdivides it, sometimes to limits beyond expectation. Like the Homeric simile, the subdivision is very tantalising (for an exemplary example read Calvino's *Invisible Cities*). For a coarser example, here is my Tom again:

> Tom couldn't look at him. The man's eyes bulged scarily. Instead, he fixed his gaze on the window to the man's left. Through the window, Tom gazed at the wide blue sky. Against the horizon he could see a large tree swaying in the breeze. High in the tallest branches, a ragged nest teetered. Sitting by the nest was the meanest-looking old black crow Tom had ever seen. But as the crow croaked and stared back at Tom, it seemed to be trying to communicate something.
>
> It was as if he was saying, Why don't you come out here with me? It's nice out here. Look, we could go for a fly into this bright blue sea of fresh air. It's free, all of it, just waiting for us.
>
> Tom shuffled nervously. Just then the crow flapped its large ragged wings and flew high into the air. Tom watched closely as the ugly bird turned effortlessly into the best kite he had ever flown. It swooped and dived and then hovered over the tree. Come with me, Tom, it seemed to say. Come with me.
>
> 'Tom,' said his mother, 'Tom?'
>
> But Tom didn't hear her. He was already moving towards the window.

This is just a mild version of the technique Calvino uses, and in no way manages to refine his use. But as you can see, beginning with the big sky, then the tree, then narrowing the vision to the crow, in subdividing the vision we can broaden the horizon of the writing without taking the story to a place it doesn't want to go.

There are other devices when considering the prose we use, but these need careful thought. Alliteration is good for the child reader (not to be confused with the oft-made mistake of Sammy Seal, Tommy Trout and so on ad nauseam – tell me you are past that stage of assuming these names are even mildly interesting). The simple alliteration in something like 'Link arms with Lola and tell her what you like' has more of a natural rhythmic resonance than 'Sammy Seal sat on the seashore.' Remember, you are writing for children, not writing *childishly*. What you are looking at is the rhythm of wordplay. Once, when I was helping a student with her Master's degree, we looked at the idea of word waltzing: writing a word and taking it for a waltz, a dance. I still like this idea a great deal: words can dance, you must have seen them, you must have heard the tune, you must have written the steps, 'Shall I compare thee to a summer's day'. Children adore the mellifluous resonance; the harmonious euphony and melodic textures of word waltzing. When writing, it is the only way the waltz really works – step, two three, one, two three . . . What I am really asking you to regard here are texture, sound, expression; words follow words into meaning and the meaningful.

We live in a multicultural, mixed-race society full of gender difference, age difference, character difference and so on. This texture is available to you. How do things feel, taste and smell? Is he as big as a mountain? Are your feelings of grief rushing through you like a tidal wave? Is her kiss as gentle as a butterfly on your lips? Did she touch you with her song? Is his heart as hard as clay on a hot summer's day? Did you weep tears of joy? Is Joy allowed to come and play? I had a friend called Joy who confessed she had never had a nickname before I called her Yoj; can you write that into your story? Is there a story there or is it just a word waltz?

Prose is about accents, rhythms, speaking voices, turns of phrase, phrasing, syntax and sound, exaggeration, minimalism, silence, the long, sweet silence that gives us time to think. In Example four (above) silence is used as a hypothetical postulate. Tom needn't show his fear. He needn't shout out his terror. He is just scared. You can do this with happy, sad, hungry, tired, woozy, warm, cold . . . Think about what you are writing again and again. Then think: Is it interesting? Is it too cluttered? Is it too sparse? Is it interesting? Where is it going? Has it done the job I want it to? Is it interesting? Have I asked this question more than once? Ask yourself why: is it interesting?

Prose is the very fabric of your narrative, weave it well for the tapestry will be a long time hanging on the wall. I know and I wish I could rewrite . . . oh, there is so much.

Finally

Just before you finally sign your book off you must remember the last rule of every children's book, which is that you *must* end with the prospect of a new beginning. What I would do with *Shooting Joe* is to suggest Josie might turn her attentions to Kazuo. It is a simple device which takes the reader down the first steps of the new life. Knowing the central character is getting on with life is your reader's payoff for sticking with the book in the first place – *the end is another beginning.*

3 Write the height

Understanding age groups

It is all too easy to say that age should not be a factor in the creative process. Good writing, a good book, a story well told will always find its reader. This is a story I have heard often, but I do not believe it.

Writing is all about knowing for whom you are writing as much as the quality of what you are writing. Writing has an audience: the literary novel (and what a self-important term that is), the airport thriller, the bodice-ripper, the ghost story, the one with the detective in a trilby, *Not Now Bernard*, the tabloid newspaper, they all have their intended audiences. What is the point in denying this? Of course, the genres leak into each other and as readers we mix and match our reading requirements. It is the same for children. But when writing for children the grading system has other rules and you must be aware of them.

In my introduction I said age and reading age are not necessarily one and the same. Intelligence and experience are not calculable in some kind of linear graph. They are more like a mosaic which is uniform in itself but denies conformity and uniformity. What ultimately matters is the receptive ability and the experience of the reader for whom you are writing. This also has to be maintained throughout the piece you are writing.

Loosely defining this is made slightly easier for us because the school system, at least initially, grades according to age. Thus, naturally, publishing tends to track this grading system. This is not infallible and I will come back to this. Nor should 'write the height' be taken literally. Think of it as a metaphor for addressing your 'target audience'.

How well do you know that audience?

As a basic rule of thumb a short 'age/fiction' table would look something like the one I have set up below. Do your own version, then research and draw up your own list of books currently in print. Visit libraries and bookshops. *Get to know what the books look like and know how they read.*

It is all about knowing reading ages and the quality of writing which caters for those ages. Evidence is there in abundance and a short sample list of suitable titles can easily be assembled but this is a job you must do yourself. There is no purpose served in me doing it for you. But remember, any book list is completely subjective. It will be a representation, not a definitive catalogue. You are not setting out to write a catalogue. Just try to get a feel for the field in which you intend to write. And if you haven't read any, I suggest you at least make a start! I repeat what I said in my introduction: It doesn't take a genius to tell you that reading more helps you to write better.

Sensory Books	**Crawling** Age 0–1	**Play with/read to** Board Books Nursery Rhymes Novelty Books
Picture Books	**Walking** Age 1–3	**Read to** Picture Books – up to 400 words
	Hopping Age 2–5	**Read to/read aloud** Picture Books – up to 1,500 words Early Readers – up to 1,000 words
	Skipping Age 4–7	**Read to/read aloud/read alone** Picture Books – up to 1,500 words Chapter Picture Books – up to 2,500 words
Short Fiction	**Running** Age 4–7	**Read to/read aloud/read alone** Picture Books – up to 1,500 words Series Fiction – up to 6,000 words Collected Short Stories – up to 1,500 words
Longer Fiction	**Racing** Age 6–9	**Read alone** Short Stories – 2,000+ words Short Novels, 12,000–20,000 words Series Fiction Collected Stories

	Dodging Age 8–11	**Read alone** Novels – 20,000–30,000 words Series Fiction
	Trekking Age 10–12	**Read alone** Pre-teen Novels – 30,000–40,000 words Series Fiction
Teen Fiction	**Flying** Age 12 +	**Read alone** Teenage Fiction – 40,000 words and counting

Note: All categories have television tie-in material, too.

As you can see, there is some leeway here on the age groupings and word counts. This table is for guidance. It is not carved in stone, but do try to research material that would fit into these categories. Reading abilities are going to vary in peer groups from the reception year onwards. That is clearly the case. But help is at hand. Increasingly publishers, especially educational publishers, are addressing this issue.

I was recently asked to submit material for a new fiction series aimed at five-, six- and seven-year-olds (years one and two, primary school). The brief was for material 'intended for the brightest third of a class'. It was recognised that within progressive reading schemes, progression by simply expecting the able child to 'reach up' to the next stage was not necessarily appropriate. It was felt that in order to keep the children interested in reading, they needed more material appropriate to their own development and experience, in order to establish themselves as readers. In simple terms, a story for a seven-year-old is not necessarily suitable for a rising five-year-old. Crucially, though, the most interesting aspect of the brief was the note that 'these children are losing interest in reading at the most critical stage'. You should never forget that writing for children carries the weight of this responsibility.

Thus, having just written a 600-word book for five-year-olds, *The Mouse Stone*, I was being asked to change and look at:

- Stories aimed at five-year-olds, at around 1,000–1,500 words
- Stories aimed at six-year-olds, at around 2,000–2,500 words
- Stories aimed at seven-year-olds, at around 4,000–5,000 words

The series is aimed at children who are 'ready to leave the basic reading schemes'. In short they were looking for material that addressed the early reading child who was ready for a challenge. Rather than pushing children to move up the age range (where subject matter becomes problematic as implied experience), material was being commissioned in a responsible and entirely appropriate manner.

Well done, those publishers.

We will now look closer at what we are writing and for whom. The implicit exercise in the above table is to get to know your reader. Before you begin writing you need to ask yourself this very simple question: *Do I know for whom I am writing?*

Every time my students write for me, I get them to specify the target age, not as an exercise in conformity, but as a small exercise in understanding needs. Invariably, in the early days of their course work they get it wrong more often than not – especially those without children of their own. But the longer they take part in the exercise the more adept they become, until they can begin to address certain vagaries within the age groupings. This has to be your target. I cannot stress strongly enough the issues here are all about understanding the child's experience and development. You are not being asked to water down your story or pay attention to politically correct trends and censorship. You *are* being asked to know your audience.

Before I go into each subsection here, I will be presenting a short critical perspective. Try not to skip this. A critical understanding of what you are approaching will serve you well.

Sensory books

Sensory Books	Crawling	Play with/read to
	Age 0–1	Board Books
		Nursery Rhymes
		Novelty Books

Sensory books – a critical perspective

It has been nearly 600 years since Copernicus discovered that the planets orbit the sun, not the other way around. Your average young child doesn't know this. I don't mean the fact itself, which is something they will eventually learn at school. I mean as a metaphor of selfhood. Actually, at this stage and until much later metaphors themselves are something they don't know much about, and we will come on to that.

As children, realising that the world doesn't revolve around us and us alone is a crucial part of our learning experience. We go from complete dependence and hopefully the nurtured attention to our every whim as babies to understanding that we are not the only people with needs. At least most of us do. Though I suspect *me, myself, I* is a fitting epitaph for many an acquaintance in all our lives – and, indeed, in ourselves from time to time, if we are honest.

The point I am making here is that, for a writer, it is useful to view this age group as going through three crucial stages, which I will call – *dependent adjusters, early activists* and *interactionists*. The crucial agenda at this age is in stimulating a child's development: stimulating thought patterns and behaviour into coherency. Sensory stimuli promoting the co-ordinating networks of interacting senses through memory encoding and repetition are all appropriate. But what does this mean to the writer?

Taken simply, what you need to know is children will learn more during their early years than they will during the rest of their lives. Eating, walking and talking is a grand oversimplification of the achievements of a brain that is developing daily, but you get the point.

Nevertheless, I do not propose to devote much space to the earliest stage, mainly because child development psychology is highly skilled and because it is also a publishing area few of us will ever work in unless we are illustrators. However, I will make a few points and offer a couple of asides.

As Nicholas Tucker reminds us, 'In the very beginning, books will mean nothing to a new baby, at the stage when even the most everyday events of life will still be sufficiently bewildering' (Tucker 1991: 23). You have all seen the books available for those children who are beginning to pay attention. There is no point dwelling on these and I will only give a few short examples. This material is easy to research and I recommend you read around the subject if you are interested because, as I will go on to show, writers often get sucked into something they don't understand.

Sensory books

Made of cloth, for example, and whose pages address sight, hearing, touch and even smell (and if they don't smell at first, they soon will). They can be made of different fibres, such as a silk patch on one page, a rubber patch on another, and have bells, electronic chimes or rustling paper inside.

Board books

In differing sizes, usually a single picture on a page, printed on hardboard that can be wiped down and is durable for grasping hands. Crucially, though, the pictures should be of colourful, whole (i.e., not abstract or with a strange perspective), recognisable objects. Don't forget this is for a child who is not even sure who the other person in the mirror is.

These can also be used to develop single-word identifications. My own son's first word was 'og!' – clearly 'frog'. Occasionally these books will follow a very slight narrative, which might be just a single word like 'apple', but at this age, these are things which parents are being encouraged to say out loud. Just as the communication skills of children need nurturing, so too do those of some adults! Of course, it is entirely possible that a child will want to return to the book for itself at a slightly later stage, perhaps even to read the word, but this depends on the longevity of the book and the book culture in households. Do not take it for granted that everyone collects books from the year dot, or that a child will read the words. Usually the reading comes after this level of book.

Often, the board book will venture into short narratives, especially nursery rhymes (see below). But it is essentially the book as an object which can be handled, with pictures, that is of use in child development. Nevertheless, I have seen board books that should be renamed 'bored'. All too often you will see board books in remainder bins and discount bookshops. This is because all too often they are published without any real perspective on child development. Recently I saw one that has a series of 'skills' to be addressed. On the left page there is a picture of a spoon with the caption 'spoon' and on the facing page, using appropriate pictures, there was the line, 'Tom takes the spoon.' This seems to be addressing adults who don't know what a child is responding to, rather than being written for the child. Besides, by the time the child has any real cognitive understanding of the spoon and its real function he or she is well into the next book stage.

The 'skills' book is innocuous enough, though. At least it promotes a parent's dialogue (and I will come on to this below). Occasionally, things go badly wrong. For example, if you ever come across a series of board books with the collected title *A Baby Driver Book*, you will see what I mean.[18] They tend to be books shaped like vehicles, a train, and a jimbo jet (no, I didn't mispell it) and so on. The machines are animated and have names, like Jimbo and Chuffie, with personalities and some fairly forced versifying to match. Not to be too unkind to their author, because a lot of work and effort went into their making, the books are totally unsuitable for the targeted audience, which becomes rather muddled.

The simple problem is one of information. Chuffie, we learn, for example, is 'a shunter', which, the author goes on to explain, is 'a steam engine from the past'. A cartoon picture of a smiling train accompanies this text. However, one needs to ask this question: how appropriate, relevant or interesting is it for a one- to two-year-old child to be fed information about a 'shunter, which is a steam engine from the past'? Of course, in no time, when they move on to *Thomas the Tank Engine*, their knowledge of shunters will be extensive. By that time, though, the children will be well past the board book stage. The series is sitting on the cusp of the board and picture book genres without really being either. And I can't begin to tell you how often this happens.

Nursery rhymes

While most of these books are very colourful, some elaborately so, the crucial element in the nursery rhyme book is the sound and rhythm when it is read or sung out loud to a child. Crucially, at this stage, it should be understood that the child is now beginning to relate to language; not necessarily the words and meanings *per se*, but the nurturing tones and a developing sense of communication. As they begin to recognise and use words the introduction of rhymes allows for development. I do not plan to dwell on this because you will not be writing them. We will look at poetry and songs later on in this book, though, which will be appropriate.

Novelty books

I love these: pop-up books, activity books, 'flap' books which encourage participation. You are going to go a long way to beat the sheer joy of Eric Carle's *Very Hungry Caterpillar*, which eats its way through the pages of the book. A little later up the age scale we can see Janet and Allan Ahlberg's *Jolly Postman*, who brings a postbag of letters for children to open and read, is ideal. Books which require a child to lift a flap to see the progress of the simplified narrative are especially encouraging and entertaining. *Kipper's Blue Balloon*, by Mick Inkpen, is a joy, too – although be prepared to see it tear. Such books are not designed to last for ever.

While these are still novelty books, we are now beginning to overlap into something else altogether. As we begin to approach the delights of books like Mick Inkpen's Kipper series and Jane Hissey's Old Bear series, which combine a narrative with the illustrations, given the right circumstances children will now be coming across their first authored book. Which is where you, as an author, will recognise that this section really begins for you – although hopefully the above information has helped you to recognise this.

Picture books

Picture Books	**Walking** Age 1–3	**Read to** Picture Books Short Story Books Television Tie-in
	Hopping Age 2–5	**Read to/read aloud** Picture Books Early Readers Short Chapter Books Television Tie-in

Skipping	Read to/read aloud/read alone
Age 4–7	Picture Books
	Early Readers
	Short Chapter Books
	Television Tie-in

Picture books – a critical perspective

It would be fair to say that the sophisticated nature of picture books gives them a special status in the literary world. A good picture book is a truly original and genuine work of art. For all of its sophistication, though, how often have we heard people snorting at the short text on each page and suggesting they could do better themselves? Even established picture-book authors, with respectable publishers, don't always get it right, and I will be looking at a couple as we proceed.

Before I go on, however, it is appropriate for me to give some critical background to the picture-book process because I feel that sometimes the desire to deconstruct and analyse a picture-book text and its processes obfuscates some of the real issues.

Much critical attention has been paid to picture books (see the bibliography). However, I am going to take issue with some of it in order to help you to understand the position from where you should be thinking about writing – and it is important you bear with me on this because it is all about writing with the knowledge of foresight.

Margaret Meek once wrote that:

> a page in a picture book is an icon to be contemplated, narrated, explicated by the viewer. It holds the story until there is a telling. So in the beginning the words are few; the story happenings are in the pictures which form polysemic text.
>
> (Meek 1988:12–13)

Commenting on this, the children's literature critic Peter Hunt said, 'Picture books, then, can develop the difference between reading words and reading pictures' (Hunt 1991: 175–88). And he invoked a quotation from another critic, Nicholas Tucker, for support: 'the art of the picture book . . . rests on the interactions between illustration and the text!' (Tucker 1991: 47). These points are all true and all well and good in their own ways. Indeed, grouped together like this, they make for coherent reading in the context in which they are presented, which is in academic texts for, principally, university undergraduate students and their tutors. Yet, I find them troublesome and want to take issue with them. Not by taking the academic high ground. On the contrary, the lower I can get, the better, as will become clear.

While these commentaries are sound and persuasive, the fact is they simply do not say enough. They do not give the really important information. Like a number of critical works on children's literature, I cannot help feeling that while the writers are sitting at the academic table, they lose sight of the child crawling under their legs. Part of the reason for this is the omission of 'nurture', which Adam Phillips addressed so eloquently and I referred to earlier. And that is not to be too hard on these three commentators, as will be discovered.

Picture books can indeed *help* to develop the difference between reading words and reading pictures. But I emphasise help, here. Because of the risk of arrest for child abuse, you should not try to experiment by plonking a child in front of such a book every day to see if the theory works. It will not, and I know Margaret Meek, Peter Hunt and Nicholas Tucker do not believe it would. Part of the reason why I have taken issue with what is written is that they *do* know this.

Their comments overgeneralise. They are not reading the height as critical experience but as an age band. They are not reading the person but critiquing the process, and there is a difference, which cannot be ignored by the writer. Unwittingly, perhaps, the critics seem to equate picture books and children of a certain age within an age-specific category, which fails to address the scale of the task.

Nicholas Tucker goes part of the way when he suggests picture books are suitable for the three to seven age group. In other books I've seen the suggestion as zero to seven. Yet, as I have already discussed and as Peter Hunt has previously suggested, pinning down a precise definition of age-related text is like chasing a chimera. But we can get closer than has been demonstrated here by looking at some other issues, which the critics have omitted in their assessment and commentary.

Think through the stages of child development! For example, consider the three to seven age group highlighted by Nicholas Tucker (1991: 46).

In the UK this age grouping comprises the following five school categories:

- Age 3   pre-school
- Age 3 to 4   nursery
- Age 4 to 5   reception
- Age 5 to 7   infants
- Age 7+   juniors

They can't all fit into one 'picture-book' group. Consider, then, how relevant this is when we also consider that the first seven years are probably the most significant learning years of a child's life. It is the period in a child's life when they will learn more than they will ever learn again. You need to go back and reconsider the 'child'. By breaking down the class size you at least have a chance to see whom you are addressing! Get to know the child. It really does pay to be alert to the possibilities. Though, once again, that's not to say everything can be easily categorised by age alone, and if I am repeating myself here then you will hopefully come to appreciate how important it is.

We have taken care of the under-twos with sensory books (although, remember, like walking and talking, age is subjective and there will be leakage). Picture books for the developing toddler immediately address the child's visual and verbal experiences but these are accompanied by the intimate nurture and shared experience of the parent/reader. And, for me, knowing this suddenly changes the strength of the picture book.

Imagine, or try to remember, that shared experience. Not as sentimentality but as an exercise in nurtured experience. There you are aged three, say, snuggled under a loved one's arm, as he/she reads *Can't You Sleep Little Bear?* – and I mention this book specifically because of the way in which it promotes the nurturing process it addresses. What we have here is a sensory event that is mediated by the reading of a book. Touch, sound, sight, story, warmth, security, affection, love; they are all brought together in the shared experience of a 'read-to' story. This is nurture in action; this is experience in the making. I am even tempted to comment that never again in our lifetime will it get better than this – although this is not my field of expertise.

In a reciprocal experience involving the parent/reader/writer/child the picture book can become the mediator.

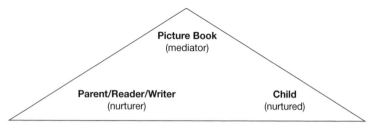

As this diagram reveals, the book can come between the nurturer/nurtured as part of the developing relationship.

Recent articles on picture books which look at critical areas in which the child breaks this cognitive experience down into differences between reading the picture and reading the words (as suggested by Perry Nodelman in Hunt (1999: 69–80)), as a process of understanding the world, seem to me to miss the initial point of the book. As mediator in a shared exercise, the above model reveals the picture book is also a much more important psychological and sociological tool. Rather than constantly looking at cognitive development, we need to try to understand how we can get involved in the process of nurture, and this is a completely different matter.

To this extent, then, deconstructing text, narrative and picture without reference to nurture seems to occur at the expense of the book and the child, never mind the experience. But surely it is all about living the experience. Even out of the home, any schoolteacher and classroom assistant will confirm this experience does not go away in schools. Indeed, the shared experience of one nurturing schoolteacher and thirty-two peer-aged children sitting on the mat at her feet has a similar effect.

Remember what Phillips said about nurture (above). Making the story connections is so much more relevant to us here. Let's consider this, then, because it is important. The picture book is not a mere 'read-to' story. It has to mediate in order to connect the parent/reader and child, and we can look at this philosophically.

In his translation of the *logos*, St Jerome said in the beginning there was the word. It was a statement eagerly grasped (and retained) by Christian theocracy. In a Western tradition and from a parental perspective of nurture, though, this translation is immediately prescriptive, authoritarian and problematic, especially when considering the experiential gap between parent and child. While a ball thrown up in the air by the child and another dropped to the ground by the parent will both be in exactly the same place at the same time, this does not mean they are going in the same direction. Modern schooling doesn't operate this Jesuit or Gragrind (as described in Dicken's *Hard Times*) method of teaching any more. Moving in the same direction has to be the aim. Try not to think of it as being a prescriptive process but a shared experience. It is when parent and child/teacher and child/writer and reader and child are all moving in the same direction. If this is being mediated through a book, then, and only then, can the writer claim to have done a good job. But how is this done? Well, it is quite simple.

Consider this, Erasmus turned St Jerome's translation around by saying the *logos* translates as, 'In the beginning was the conversation', which is an altogether more intimate discourse (and perhaps we can see why early theocracy rejected its lack of authority). The storyteller who can engage with an audience through pictures, words and actions, bringing the audience along with the story, is one who understands the craft of storytelling. The 'picture book' *logos* then becomes an experience of nurtured reason, expressed through words, pictures and the entire intimate, shared sensory event – the balls have to be going in the same direction. But as a writer you have to be careful. The trouble with juggling is the balls always go where you throw them. You have to practise the craft. You have to know the best way to bounce the words. There is no point in just tossing them in the air and hoping they land right, for they rarely do.

Thus, your job as a writer is not to sit at the desk and try to talk at the children. Before you attempt to tease a story out of your creative self, you need to know where the children are, to get down and join them, especially your youngest picture-book readers. When writing for this age, your job is to provide a book that draws all of these nurture issues together.

Further, I know this is not a critical exposition, but every parent/teacher/helper/babysitter in the world knows that even the worst day with a 'terrible two-year-old' is rendered worthwhile at this point. Crucially, though, it is for the child, too. The right book, a favourite, good story, is also the point of mediation and a chance to negotiate a domestic truce, before re-establishing the loving bond. Those lucky enough to have experienced it for themselves should take a moment to reflect and try to analyse why they still hanker for it. Those who never experienced it can reflect on why they want to help others foster it by writing such a book. It really is that simple. Get to know how the book functions. I'm not about to tell you whether I am reflecting on actual or missed experience here. There have to be some secrets between us. But I will tell you that, however successful you are, part of your own reason for writing for children ought to be dedicated to the nurture process and the ability to promote shared experience.

But be honest about it. Children's books are not about misplaced sentimentality – that is the domain of adults. As Bruno Bettelheim has written, 'It destroys the value of the fairy tale for the child if someone details its meaning for him' (Bettelheim 1976: 69). This is just as true for the story you are about to write. The child doesn't need the contrite or the mawkishness of the overly sentimental, which they rarely understand in any case.

This brings me to the most important piece of advice in this whole book:

Write *for* children – not at them!

The rightly celebrated children's author/illustrator Maurice Sendak has been quoted as saying, 'I am trying to draw the way children *feel* – or rather, the way I imagine they feel' (Tucker 1991: 49). Taken in this context, that is as a quotation isolated from the rest of the interview, I don't know which of the two things he is trying to do is worse.

Which of us wants to receive a book that clones rather than moves or stimulates us? Surely books are written to *make* us feel. Written to stimulate our understanding of feelings, reason and experience. Written to nurture and help us understand those feelings when we feel them. Actually I think Maurice Sendak achieves this quite brilliantly: he just didn't articulate it very well (at least not in the way he has been quoted here). Which just goes to show the practitioner isn't necessarily the best describer of his own work. If we add to this the fact that the critic isn't necessarily the best disseminator either, we can at least have some understanding of what we are trying to address.

When Jacqueline Rose (1994: 12) wrote, 'childhood persists . . . as something we endlessly rework in our attempt to build an image of our own history', she was talking about us adults and our perception of our childhood pasts. Nevertheless, the child who is the picture-book receptor is not living childhood as a history but as a present. Children live and think in real time. Reflection, nostalgia and memory recall are psychological developments. We have to try to reach out to children, as they live in this real time, but this does not mean we should try to be them. This, surely, is the logic of the picture book. It is also why 'flashback' never works in the picture-book medium – it is something a child this young does not comprehend. But in writing the picture book we must bring to life and stimulate the passivity of the child's imagination for a child who cannot yet visualise a future. So we stimulate the projection of a future, not by regurgitating the past or the eversame present, but by providing a promise of what life can offer. To this end, then, we can look at one of Jacqueline's Rose's most astute observations: 'Language is not [just] something which we use to communicate' (*ibid.*: 16). In addressing the young child, it is a promissory note for the future, which in time they will come to recognise is a projection of the present.

Given the right environment, a nurtured child will develop such cognitive understanding but only if it is part of the reading process. As Jack Zipes says, 'Storytellers cannot and should not pretend to be therapists, gurus or social workers' (Zipes 1995: 223). I come back to Adam Phillips – all we can do is help to make the connections, where nurture is the key.

Further, the picture book is indeed a major resource for the development of a child's sensory perception. But when did you as an adult ever think about your perception as something which is split into differences between sight and sound, say? Everyday life for us, *homo fabula, homo historia*, is a polysemic experience in a polyphonic world, which becomes part of our own life's story. Unlike President Ford (it is rumoured), we can walk and chew gum at the same time – and from a very early age, too. This age group will have no problem, given the right encouragement.

As you can see, then, there is nothing simple about the simple little picture book.

Picture Books	**Walking**	**Read to**
	Ages 1–3	Picture Books
		Short Story Books
		Television Tie-in

Having recognised the need to address the age groups in specialised areas, you will also recognise the specialised nature of text required. In reading the height you will need to look at length, language and the subject matter that can bridge the gap between the big reader and the little listener. Get the height of your child firmly in your head as you begin your story, but remember that the story has to be worth telling. I have seen so many picture-book texts that remind me of shopping lists. Ask yourself this: would you read a list for pleasure?

Don't be fooled into thinking the picture book is a quick way into writing – especially if that thought is premised on the idea that you only have to write a few hundred rather than thousands of words. A good picture book is probably the most difficult book to write. My students certainly find it one of the hardest disciplines to master and many never do, mainly because you only have a limited word count in which to tell a *big* story.

A picture book is not a little story, or a short story for children. As Diana Kimpton (2000) has said so eloquently, a picture book is 'a long story told short'. And that quotation, summing up such a big topic, says much about the economy of text, which does not come at the expense of the information it conveys.

As I said above, a child needs the same ingredients for a story as does an adult. They need a character around whom the story, with its acutely plotted beginning, middle and end, unfolds. And as I explained, we must see the central character develop. To which I will add it should always be human, whether it is a mouse, a monkey or Percy the Park Keeper. The character has to be one a child can identify with (even if he or she can't identify it). Rarely do creatures who do not know what they are or inanimate objects work. Exceptions like *Thomas the Tank Engine* and the trucks in *Bob the Builder* are often assisted by television to gain success.

Past success counts for little either, though. Martin Waddell's seminal *Can't You Sleep Little Bear?* did him no favours when he came to write *A Kitten Called Moonlight*, which on opening breaks some very basic rules of picture-book writing and never recovers. It must have seemed like a good idea when conceived but the execution is extremely poor because neither the text nor the pictures work, together or apart. After reading it (and I urge you to do so) try to figure out where *A Kitten Called Moonlight* goes wrong.

One of the biggest unwritten rules in picture-book writing is a simple one. *Picture books are written in real time!*

It seems an extraordinarily simple principle, but if picture books are to become like a mediator in a conversation with a child, understanding this is very important. Issues like flashback, which many children don't understand in any case. Yesterday, last year, tomorrow, next week are still very obscure ideas for very young children to grasp. This doesn't mean you cannot set your story over a couple of days, but the child has to be able to see time through their relationship with it – like through breakfast, lunch, dinner and bedtime, for example. But once again, do your own research on this.

Length

There are two major things to consider here: the number of pages and the number of words.

Page count

Picture books are typically 32 pages long, including 2 pages for the title and imprint. This leaves you with a minimum of 24 pages, or 12 double spreads, up to a maximum of 30 pages, or 15 double spreads, to work to. However, I say typically because occasionally a publisher will specify a different length requirement – especially in the education market. Recently I have written for 24- and 48-page picture books. The illustration on page 100 reveals a typical model for a 32–page book.

As you can see, the 12 double spreads could be pushed to 13 and 14 with judicious use of the end papers, but it is unlikely. However, you can also see from the illustration that it is crucial to consider each single page or double spread (more usual for this grouping) as a different scene to keep the story moving forward. Read it like a film moving from scene

1	2	3	4	5
End Board	End Paper	End Paper	Prelims	Title Page

6	7	8	9	10	11
Double	spreads	moving	two	by	two
12	13	14	15	16	17
18	19	20	21	22	23
24	25	26	27	28	29

30	31	32
End Paper	End Paper	End Board

to scene. I always mock one up so that I can chart the changes and try to gauge the page-turning ideas, like cliff–hanger page endings and suchlike. Don't think mock-up is just a child's game. It helps you to get hang of the idea that a picture book is about page-turning scenes. It's simple to do, too. Take 8 pieces of A4 paper and fold them in 2 to make a 32-page book. Then enter your text as appropriate. Make sure each double spread produces a new scene. It is important to get this into your head and use the mock-up to try to see your book.

A good picture book is not just written; it is constructed, grown even. Illustrators, like the talented Ian Beck, always make mock–ups. If the illustrator ends up playing around with your suggested page breaks, that is something you will have to bear. However, it won't be gratuitous fiddling. The illustrator will just see the book differently. Besides, at this stage the book is getting made. How much say you want to have will all depend on your relationship with the publisher. Furthermore, the illustrator has to be trusted to visualise your words. Remember, he or she is an artist, too, only working in a different medium.

Word count

Picture books vary greatly. Anything from a word a page to 1,500 words is considered acceptable. For this younger age group the word count is usually on the low side. I recently revisited two old favourites in our house: *Jasper's Beanstalk*, by Nick Butterworth and Mick Inkpen, has only 92 words; *Kipper*, by Mick Inkpen, has 328 words. Yet, both tell equally relevant stories and stand on the same 'age' shelf (one to three) very suitably. If your word count is creeping over 500 at this lower age group you are probably writing for the wrong height. Good research will reveal this, though. Once again, do your own study. Get to know what you want to write. But you have to understand that the low word count isn't a dogmatic trend. It is all about maintaining the attention span of the child for whom you are writing.

Language

This is something that can vary. The aim of every picture book is to present a complete and coherent idea in as few words as possible. Every single word must count. Avoid any unnecessary padding, whimsy and off-hand comments. Make every word count to drive the story forward. And remember, too, it has to be a story. I'm quite sure publishers have had their fill of lists of events which become more like a child's story rather than a story for a child – and you must be aware of the difference. Also, allow the pictures room to complement the text. The best gift a writer can give is space for the illustrated joke. When I wrote *The Mouse Stone* I ended the story with a joke, then gifted it to the illustrator, George Hollingworth. George will get all the credit, but who cares? The result is worth the effort for the child. The child is worth the effort.

But this picture/text balance can only be accomplished if the text is kept sparse. While the text is short, though, it has to be able to stand alone as a complete story. No illustrator, however great, will ever be able to make up for an inadequate or mediocre narrative. Keep sentences short and simple so the pictures can breathe life into them. Also keep the sentences short and simple because the text has to be read out loud.

Crucially, it is the book's *concept* which comes to dominate. If the concept is right the words and pictures will soon follow. And don't think the concept needs to be that simple, either. Judy Waite's book *Mouse Look Out* won the English Association's prize for the best picture book of 1999 but it is a very dark story about an exploring mouse being tracked by a cat, who doesn't see the dog behind it. Never think children are frightened by challenging text; the only thing that scares them off is bad text.

Story bridge

To bridge the story from the parent/reader to the child is the big challenge of the book if it is to mediate.

Try to think of the text in terms of pictures. The last time you visited the cinema or watched television you might have noticed that the action taking place is not explained through the dialogue. Rather, the picture and dialogue combine to create an overall impression. The same goes for the picture book. But, generally, at the simpler end of the scale the clues and connections are more obvious.

Take Sally Grindley and Clive Scrutton's *Four Black Puppies*, for example. It is a very simple narrative of four pups waking up and slowly exploring their environment. The text explains much of what is happening when the pups begin to wander around. Nevertheless, the breadth of the pictorial text gives a wider story which reveals what the pups are doing in a wider context. It is this wider context you have to consider. The narrative text, 'One shopping basket falling down . . .', hardly describes the mayhem and havoc being wreaked around the house when the four pups get going – as revealed by the picture.

The wider context and concept of the book allow the child to see the cause, effect and consequence of certain seemingly innocuously playful actions. In *Jasper's Beanstalk* when Jasper plants his bean even a child who has no experience of things growing can relate it to things that grow. Eventually, the connection will become apparent. But the concise narrative, linked to the picture, allows the cognitively developing child to understand that words alone do not tell the whole story. I repeat something I have written elsewhere: 'children can understand much more than they can articulate or express and not to recognise this is an abuse that ends up being detrimental to their development' (Melrose 2000: 35).

Similarly, a child with developing cognition skills can see more than they can articulate, so they react to the visual. The fact that they cannot say, 'Those are really naughty pups', when looking at *Four Black Puppies* does not mean they do not understand how careless the pups are. The lack of words in relation to the picture should not be seen as textually detrimental.

So work out a strong concept, such as a child of the relevant experience can relate to, keep the story narrative short and let the illustrator have all the best jokes. It will still be your story.

On the issue of story, a good thing to think about for this age is the 'rule of three', cue *Rumplestiltskin, Goldielocks and the Three Bears et al.* The symmetry of three, coinciding with beginning, middle and end, keeps the heightened tension of the story going forward. There is little chance of the story sagging if the quest is concluded only after the third attempt, for example; and, indeed, early failure is developmental in terms of character and plotting. How does your character respond to failure? To give up loses the story; to persevere is dramatic. Of course, repetitions in threes in the text are effective, too. 'I'll huff and I'll puff and I'll blow your house down,' works well in *The Three Little Pigs*.

Once you have this story, go through it repeatedly, look to revise and rewrite it. Believe me, it will need it! I said earlier try to make a little mock-up. This helps us to see the page turning as part of the storytelling process. But it is very important to read it out loud. This will help you to locate any clumsy writing, loose alliteration, dodgy rhythm, creaky sentences, lost sense and nonsense. Once, when the daughter of a friend of mine came home from school with a friend, the friend asked, 'What does your dad do in there?' His daughter answered, 'He talks to himself.' You, too, need to talk to yourself. Then, after you have revised, revised and revised, try reading it to someone else. Better still, get someone else to read it out loud to you. When you hear it read back as it appears on the page, rather than with your *imagined* inflection and delivery, it can be a real shock – but what a good exercise in editing it is.

Presentation

Curiously, the question I get asked more than any other is: how do I present a picture-book text for a publisher? I say curiously because it should be the last consideration. If you think you have the perfect idea, appraise it again. Then and only then, after you are really ready, should you think about sending it to anyone. Try to be sure about your story, though. I recently listened to a picture-book idea from someone who has been writing successfully for children for over thirty years and there is no way it would ever work. This is mainly because it referred to a school craze, which was already going out of fashion in the UK. Further, because of the cost involved in making picture books, publishers inevitably look for an internationally translatable story. The craze I refer to was international but crazes peak and trough at different times throughout the world, so it is hard to anticipate how the book will sell when it is not solely relying on the text alone.

On the subject of illustration, the popularity of Shirley Hughes serves as a timely reminder that there are very few of us who can illustrate and write with equal ability. You do not have to illustrate your story. Nor do you have to find an illustrator. If you have a good story, a publisher will find you an illustrator.

When presenting a picture-book manuscript to an editor, I find it is a good idea to send two versions. The first is the story split into page numbers, but just giving the straight story narrative:

Title	A *Picture Book*
Page 1	Cover Page
Pages 2–3	End Papers
Page 4	Prelims: Dedication
Page 5	Title Page
Double Spreads	
Pages 6–7	(text . . .)
Pages 8–9	(. . .)

Pages 10–11   (…)
Pages 12–13   (…)
Pages 14–15   (…)
Pages 16–17   (…)
Pages 18–19   (…)
Pages 20–21   (…)
Pages 22–23   (…)
Pages 24–25   (…)
Pages 26–27   (…)
Pages 28–29   (…)
Pages 30–31   (…)
Page 32   Cover Page

Then enclose another version, which includes some picture ideas. These need only be thumbnail word sketches in italics, just to give the editor a broader perspective. For example:

> Pages 6–7   (*Danny looks startled as a big dinosaur stares down at him.*) When Danny opened his eyes the dinosaur was still there!

As the age grouping begins to move on, so too does the perception of the child and I want will say a little more about this before we continue with short fiction. However, before I proceed I want to say more about the 'picture-book experience' and to explain this to you in a way you can imagine for yourself. If we look at what pleases us we will have a better idea of what pleases others. Yet, so many writers do not pay attention to this. Try to relate to this 'sensory exercise' yourself, before thinking about a third party (such as a child), because the experience has the ability to engage all our senses at the same time.

I first began writing this section at 6 a.m. on a cold January morning. And I was trying to imagine (daydreaming, probably) what kind of 'picture-book experience' I, as an adult, would appreciate – at least one I could put into print here. What would help me to experience that sense of blissful wellbeing and security? Bearing in mind it is 6 a.m. and cold, let me try to share that thought with you, because hopefully it will enable you to channel something like it into your knowledge of what is being experienced by a child. In an effort to describe a multi-sensory experience, this is what I typed:

I am sitting under the pergola, easing out the crick in my neck after a long day at the computer, where I write. I have a glass of Chianti in one hand and a small bowl of fat black olives close by the other. I'm fiddling for the olives, not looking, because I am distracted by something else I can see. My fingers touch the bowl, then the olives and I pop one into my mouth, spit out the stone and sip the plum-skin-purple wine. The heady wisteria waving near by confuses the scent of the wine as it washes the bitter olive away with a burst of chocolate-textured, damson and vanilla fruit. Before me the towers of San Gimignano are silhouetted against the bright yellow, red and orange hues of a Tuscan sunset. The crick in my neck is fading with the light. The sky begins to melt into pink and purple. It's too early for the fireflies but the crickets are already in full chorus. Behind me, *Coro a bocca chiusa* hums discreetly from the stereo, interrupted only by a squeal, 'Come on, Dad, are we going swimming or not?' As I stand up I can smell a pesto sauce simmering in the pan. A swim before dinner sounds a very good idea indeed.

Och (as we say where I come from), sentimental rubbish, but go and write your own ten seconds. For that is all we are talking about, not much more. It's just a moment in time in which sight, sound, taste, smell, touch and emotions come together. The point I am trying to get you to acknowledge and regard is the 'picture-book experience' as a multi-accentual, polysemic idea of bliss, jouisance – a shared moment when a story can become the focus for an easily distracted attention span. No sentimental description of it (like mine) will ever replace it as experience. Your book has to become part of the experience. You cannot just think of it as something to read or be read or looked at and enjoyed. It can be so much more in the nurture process and you will do well to remember this.

What you have to remember is you are writing for the inexperienced child who can already eat, watch television, daydream, ask for a *fromage frais* to be opened, scratch an itch, kick a comic on the floor, reject the cabbage, bang the table with a spoon, sip some water, decide not to go to the toilet, change his name to Squirtle, shout and smile and change his mind in the time it has taken you to blink. This polymath in polyester clothing isn't some alien fiend. It is childhood as it has always been (apart from the polyester).

Moving back to the book, then, having recognised the needs of the one to three age group, we can now move on to the two to fives as a specialised area, although it encroaches on the early reader, too.

Hopping	**Read to/read aloud**
Age 2–5	Picture Books
	Early Readers
	Short Chapter Books
	Television Tie-in
Skipping	**Read to/read aloud/read alone**
Age 4–7	Picture Books
	Early Readers
	Short Chapter Books
	Television Tie-in

At this stage, we are still dealing with the picture book and you will also recognise the specialised nature of text required. In reading the height, once again you will need to look at length, language and the subject matter that can bridge the gap between the big reader and the little listener or early reader. Nevertheless, once again get the story clearly into your head. Sorry to be repetitive, but needs must.

Length

Once again there are two major things to consider here: the number of pages and the number of words on the page.

Pages

As above, 32 pages, 12–15 double spreads, still applies. Although recently I have been asked for a 48-page text as an early picture-book reader. It is still crucial to consider each single page and each double spread as presenting a different scene. The golden rule is to keep the story moving forward.

Word count

At this age picture books vary greatly. For example, guidelines from Walker Books suggest they vary in length from 100 to 3,000 words. Random House suggest 1,500 words maximum. In my experience, a maximum of 900 words is a good average for a picture book. But your story need only be as long as it is. As long as a piece of string and as short as a shadow will do if the story is complete. The 48-page one I am writing now is around 900 words, even with the extra page length. And recent educational requests for the same age group (four to five) are asking for anything between 600 and 1,200 words.

Let me just say something on word counts, though. They are restrictive and problematic. The best idea is to get your story shaped first then worry about the word count in the redrafting. It can take me no time at all to write a first draft but then weeks to get the final version (months on the latest one I am working on).

Remember Diana Kimpton's advice: a picture book is not a little story but a big story told short.

Language

Once again, this is something that can vary. But the aim stays the same as with the younger group. Every picture book has to present a complete and coherent idea in as few words as possible. Every single word must count. For this 'height', though, you have a little more space to develop the story.

You must still avoid any unnecessary padding, fickle, over-fancy and offhand comments. These will slow down the story. But you can be a little more lyrical, realistic or magical in your presentation of the narrative. Once again, allow the pictures room to complement the text. This can only be accomplished if the text is kept sparse.

Also, it's important to remember that simile, metaphor, ellipses, flashback and an overreliance on explanation will not work in the picture-book medium. *Picture books work in real time!* I have rarely if ever seen a flashback work in this medium. It is important to remember this because children live in real time. And if I am repeating myself again, so be it. It needs to be said time and again.

A couple of other tips. Ask yourself whether you have given words where a picture would tell the story better. Ask yourself if you have changed viewpoint (because you shouldn't). While the two agendas of Big Bear and Little Bear in *Can't You Sleep Little Bear?* are obvious, the text does not change viewpoint. It is simply the case that Barbara Firth's pictures manage to represent both viewpoints (and see the section on 'Viewpoint', above). Make sure you know what your story is. All too often I see two stories getting mixed together. The storyline has to be a strong, linear narrative. Recently I read a complaint that publishers send picture-book texts back with a fairly standard rejection that usually says the story is 'not strong enough'. The complaintant asked what this means. The answer is simple: the story has to be a big story! As Robert McKee (1999: 20) has written, 'Good story means something worth telling that the world wants to hear. Finding this is your lonely task.' Nevertheless, through stories, there is much you as a writer can do to assist in developing the world you will be representing.

Also, get to know what the different ages need in terms of experience, subject matter and cultural diversity. Then, when you finally finish your story, read it out loud, preferably to an adult friend (children, especially your own, do not make impartial judges). Then consider things like: is the text working? How long does it take to read? Is the story the right length, too short, or too long? You can tell a big story short. Even with a funny punchline, few of us speak 900 words at a time.

Fiction

Short Fiction	**Running** Age 4–7	**Read to/read aloud/read alone** Picture Books – up to 1,500 words Series Fiction – up to 6,000 words Collected Short Stories – up to 1,500 words Television Tie-in
Longer Fiction	**Racing** Age 6–9	**Read alone** Short Stories 2000+ words Short Novels, 12,000–20,000 words

Series Fiction
Collected Stories
Television Tie In

Dodging Age 8–11	**Read alone** Novels – 20,000–30,000 words Series Fiction
Trekking Age 10–12	**Read alone** Pre-teen Novels – 30,000–40,000 words Series Fiction

Teen Fiction	**Flying** Age 12+	Teenage Fiction – 40,000 words and counting

Fiction for children – a critical perspective

It is often assumed that fiction for children is the easiest to write and get published. Certainly the scope is there. Anything from 500 to 50,000 words can come into the picture and I hope the above chart is useful. Some of the most famous children's writers can and do make a very good living out of writing short, rather than long, pieces. (Although do not expect to make a living out of writing for children. If you do, consider it to be a bonus. Very few manage to make it a full-time occupation.) When you are writing fiction it is as well to consider what Fred Inglis has argued:

> it is simply ignorant not to admit that children's novelists have developed a set of conventions for their work. Such development is a natural extension of the elaborate and implicit system of rules, orthodoxies, improvisations, customs, forms and adjustments that characterise the way any adult tells stories or simply talks at length to children.
>
> (Inglis 1981: 101)

While it can be established that some early examples of what has come to be recognised as children's literature, such as *The Wind in the Willows* and *Treasure Island*, may not have been written specifically with children in mind, those doubts no longer exist. With only a very few exceptions, books these days are written specifically for children and Fred Inglis is right, 'conventions' have become implicit in the writing of them. Yet, while conventions themselves are implicit, they are also multifarious and complex and you must not let them stifle your creativity. A good story is a good story; you just have to think carefully about who best will benefit from it. Just to repeat what is fast becoming a mantra, tailor the story to fit the audience by writing the height. A good novel for an eight-year-old can be spoiled because the language is too complex (or too simple). It is not the story that is the problem but the way it is told, although, of course, I do not need to tell you the subject matter is an equally important consideration.

But in thinking about fiction for children, there seems no sense in me getting involved in a 'whither literature' type discussion here. As an old-fashioned post-structuralist in my academic life, the urge to get involved in this kind of debate seems to me to be largely irrelevant to a book of this nature. Nevertheless, I do believe an understanding of critical positioning has allowed me to look at children's fiction objectively and this is something you need to consider. An objective point of view will help your subjectivity. And I concur with Robert Leeson when he states that children's literature

> is special literature . . . its writers have special status in home and school, free to influence without direct responsibility for upbringing and care. This should not engender irresponsibility – on the contrary. It is much a matter of respect, on the one hand for the fears and concerns of those who bring up and educate children, and on the other for the creative freedom of those whose lives are spent writing for them. I have generally found in discussion with parents or teachers, including those critical of or hostile to my work, that these respects are mutual.
>
> (Leeson 1985: 169–70)

This responsibility is also why writing for children is not simpler than writing for adults. If anything, it is harder because there are many more things to consider, especially when we remember (and we should never forget) that children are vulnerable, impressionable and open to manipulation, which they ought to be protected from. Yet, to what extent should this set of criteria be taken into account? For example, it is still difficult to gauge whether certain literature is harmful to children or not. Let us consider this.

Few, for example, would claim to have suffered harm from the works of C.S. Lewis,[19] whose 'career as a misanthrope, misogynist, xenophobe, and classroom bully has been well and depressingly documented' (Goldthwaite 1996: 223) and this case is not really up for debate. Yet, clearly, in reading Lewis's books, the ideological positioning is something that is hard to ignore. As Andrew Blake has observed,

> Even if we disapprove of Lewis's politics, we are discussing here a popular author; in particular one still widely read and admired by children, who presumably internalise . . . [his] hierarchical and patriarchal views, and possibly even sympathise with them, as they look for positive outcomes from the stories. What we cannot do is ignore this. Indeed we should study the work of C.S. Lewis, in order to work towards an understanding of his academic, literary and theological conservatism, and towards a clearer understanding of his times.
>
> (Blake 2000: 53)

Clearly, while Lewis's books are still popular, and ripe for academic research, as Andrew Blake says, all 'too often even the most cynical or historically informed reader is brought up hard against the very limited boundaries of Lewis's world-view' and the subject of his books simply has 'nothing to do with contemporary widely travelled, hybrid, multicultural Britain, or indeed anywhere else' (*ibid.*). In which case, while we may study Lewis's work as presenting a contextualised retrospective of a deeply disturbing and anachronistic ideology, his continuing success suggests his core ideas, while offensive to any liberally inclined person, are not something we can take for granted – especially when they are directed at children.

I would suggest we do not take them for granted. With the obvious exception of Lewis's publishers, publishing in the Western world now seems to be regulating the very things he is guilty of. This is part of the implicit convention currently in force.

At the beginning of this new millennium, most of the evidence reveals that writers and publishers have for the past twenty years or so been reflecting a cultural and ideological shift towards intolerance for such writing. To which it might be added that this shift in emphasis seems to have come as a result of a more responsible awareness of what is deemed appropriate for children. Lewis is undoubtedly a writer of some strength and of no uncertain style and charm, but his clunking combination of racism, sexism and prominent Christian[20] apologetics manages to set up a curious set of unwholesome paradoxes that would be anachronistic in books being written today. Indeed, they were problematic even in his own time, and Nicholas Tucker has suggested that '[Lewis's] Christian doctrines of atonement and resurrection . . . sometimes push the plot into directions that seem cruel and illogical' (Tucker 1991: 100) and I tend to agree with this assessment.

However, suggesting current publishing rejects this doctrinal writing also suggests that the twenty-first-century child is currently being treated to material that is going through a form of liberal censorship. Not from a strict, autocratic source, but as a discourse of cultural progress – and while I use the word progress from a personal positioning, it surely has to be viewed as progress that we are more aware of the problems that can cause more than just offence.

Saying out loud that if the Narnia books were being written today it is pretty certain that Lewis wouldn't be published is a notion likely to be met with incredulity in many areas, and I have certainly come across this in Europe and the USA. But it is also fairly certain that if Lewis was indeed writing books today, he would probably not write the way he did back in the forties and fifties. This is simply because his racist, sexist, theological and autocratic ordering is a discourse of its time and (it has to be hoped) has only limited appeal these days. Even the most conservative among us must accept it is not entirely wholesome for our children to be challenged in this way, without their having the benefit of experience that allows them at least to question it.

Nevertheless, this does not mean to say that you, as writer, can ignore these issues. And I am not here referring to the insulting term politically correct, but to the maintenance of a creative vigilance in which the creation of a utopia can just as easily be another's hell; adding the caveat, if we have accepted such material in the past, we can and will again. Thus, as writers, we have to remember that we have a responsibility over what we write. I agree with Andrew Blake that writers like Lewis should be studied so that the issues they address can be contextualised. And I also agree with him when he writes: 'study . . . will shed light on the continuing success of a writer whom liberal and left-inclined literary opinion – usually intent on chasing utopias of its own – can too easily dismiss as an anachronism' (Blake 2000: 59). Clearly, Lewis's popularity points to the ongoing problem. Unsuitable material must be addressed at the time of writing. It should not need retrospective, academic research to have to reveal the baneful masquerading as moral when it is already too late, because it will always be too late for the children's sake. Abuse is about more than bruises and this should always be at the back of your mind when writing for the impressionable.

I cannot tell you what to write. Nor can I ask you to write what I would prefer. You must search your own conscience to consider what writing is appropriate for a morally responsible, multicultural society. Try to remember, when you are writing, you have already lived much longer than your reader has. You have the experience to distinguish between the rubbish and the real. You have the critical wherewithal to filter out the pernicious and your own prejudices.

But as I have said before, censorship is all about power and control, and, as far as I can tell, moral majorities are just as dangerous as cultural revolutionists are. And, I might add, I would never advocate the banning of books by writers like Lewis. Since Lewis considered that a children's story was the best art form for expressing something you feel you have to say, he may have been aware he was saying some contentious things to the very audience who could not speak back. And indeed that 'something to say' may have a jackbootish leaning, but burning books has its own history, which I could never condone. Better that children grow up knowing, as Andrew Blake has suggested, that something virulent lurks in the weft and warp which can be addressed in an intelligent manner, so that future authors are aware of its otherwise hidden potential. Further, we adults should not assume we are giving children what they want without knowing what they need and vice versa. Being a grown-up does not make your opinion empirically verifiable. As a writer you have a responsibility to remember this and you are not always going to get it right. None of us do. But if we maintain a creative vigilance (see Melrose 2000) in our writing we will have a better chance of getting it right, and surely this has to be desirable.

I do not believe creativity can or should be stifled by a sense of awareness. The reason I used Lewis in my example is due to two things. First, he knew what he was doing, it was a calculated job. Second his work is promoted by adults with a blind faith that needs watching. For example, assuming a Christian premise must be wholesome seems to be misplaced. This is precisely the kind of issue that should be scrutinised, and I make no apology for having done so. In *Rasselas* Samuel Johnson wrote, 'Be not too hasty, to trust, or admire, the teachers of morality: they discourse like angels, but they live like men.' This goes for all of us. It is important if we are not to reproduce misplaced, inappropriate literature for a vulnerable audience. And the net can be cast wide. I recently heard Nicholas Tucker and Jack Zipes, two prominent commentators on children's literature, debating the issue of possible sexism in the Harry Potter books.[21] While it has to be said that Zipes's overstatements on the subject came off worse in the debate, the suggestion that there are some sexist issues remaining to be addressed seems flimsy. The Harry Potter series is slightly retrograde in its portrayal of a Gothic fantasy in old-school stories and the sexist potential is obvious in such stories. Nevertheless, while the stories rely on some gender-specific issues, so too does real life and they cannot be ironed out completely if some sense of realism is to be retained. I am quite sure the issues of sexism are not going to be too challenged by Harry Potter. Besides, there are a number of strong female characters to be confronted, too.

Although, having promised a new-found kid-lit-liberalism, I have just read Anthony Horowitz's book *Stormbreaker*, and the racial stereotyping of the bad guys, Herod Sayle and his sidekicks, harks back to another less pluralistic and multicultural age. Like Nicholas Tucker, I think children's attraction to issues such as these is more complex than our adult understanding of it and clearly this cannot be anything other than an introduction to a debate for another book. The point has, I think, been made. *It is take care!* As I have written elsewhere,

> To dress . . . stories up . . . in a dubious, poorly considered moral tale with a forced happy ending is artifice verging on mendacity. But just as bad, as I have already explained, rather than opportunism, it could just as easily be ignorance misconstrued . . . Knowing and thinking you know what makes story authentic is not the same thing. Good intentions do not necessarily lead to good stories.
>
> (Melrose 2001: 36)

To ignore this, to collude with the paucity of judgement being exercised, is to abrogate all moral responsibility. We cannot simply refuse to condemn systems of thought that are being presented in a reckless, agenda-laden manner. Even from this small example it is clear that you can write any old thing you choose, although you do need to consider whether a child should be reading it. I can't stress the importance of this enough. Lewis's accomplishments (for example) do not make up for his deficiencies, and most of his child readers are too young and inexperienced to know this. You *must* consider this at the time of writing.

Considering the moral issues is an interesting exercise. For example, much work has been done on fairy tales, their traditional use as stories and our relationship with them. Take the story of Little Red Riding Hood, for example. The story is multidimensional and complex. It could be said that it is a warning to newly menstruating young girls (signified by the red hood) not to go into the forest where they might encounter the Big Bad Wolf, but this is simplistic. It could equally be read as 'men's fear of women's sexuality and of their own as well . . . The curbing and regulation of sexual drives [are] fully portrayed in the bourgeois literary fairy-tale on the basis of deprived male needs. Red Riding Hood is to blame for her own rape' (Zipes 1997: 81). In other words the little girl should know better than to flaunt herself in front of the primordial man. But what happens when this idea is replicated in novels? What chance Hardy's Tess, in *Tess of the D'Urbervilles*, for example? What hope as she is sent by her feckless father to seek out his family honour? Tess leaves the family home, described thus:

> She put on her white frock . . . the airy fullness of which, supplementing her enlarged *coiffure*, imparted to her developing figure an amplitude which belied her age, and might cause her to be estimated as a woman when she was not much more than a child.
>
> (Hardy 1983: 52)

Like Little Red Riding Hood, she is entering the forest in unfamiliar attire. Only to return pregnant to deliver some of the saddest words ever written in fiction:

> 'O mother, my mother!' cried the agonised girl . . . 'How could I be expected to know? I was a child when I left this house four months ago. Why didn't you tell me there was danger in men-folk? Why didn't you warn me? Ladies know how to fend hands against, because they read novels that tell them of these tricks; but I never had the chance o' learning in that way, and you did not help me.'
>
> (*Ibid.*: 87)

As Hardy readily exposes, the issue of blame is a fraught one. Nevertheless, how like a man to expect the lesson to be learned in a novel. To say that Hardy has written some of the most obsequiously obnoxious men in literature is a personal viewpoint, but if anyone can think of anything good to say about Alex D'Urbervilles and Angel Claire I would like to hear it justified. Yet, his reading of Little Red Riding Hood is implicit here.

Poor Tess, meantime, if she had only known the Little Red Riding Hood story, far less having read the kind of novel she claims she should have had access to. (Indeed, we can see a clumsy, authorial intervention taking place here. How else would she have known novels she *never* read contain the information? Of course, Richardson's *Pamela* and *Clarissa*, written the century before, might have helped.) On the subject of the rape of both Little Red and Tess, though, Hardy's clumsy explanation at the end of 'The Maiden' and just prior to 'Maiden no More' in

Tess of the D'Urbervilles, where he highlights the inevitability of the situation, brought on by centuries of abuse, is no justification. And the lesson Hardy hands out is highly questionable as guidance to young girls. Hardy admits this but offers no solution throughout the remaining 300 pages, except to suggest, in many more words, that Tess (Little Red Riding Hood) was to blame for her own rape. Now where have I heard that before? And while it is easy to dismiss these as just stories, mere fiction, it is the underlying discourse and attempted justification that are important. Hardy's Tess, like Little Red Riding Hood, was just too sexy for her own good, which exposes the acceptance of male sexual dominance in the cultural context. Just like Lewis's problems, we cannot ignore what may be implicitly contained in our writing. We must be careful when writing it.

Still, I also find myself agreeing with C.S. Lewis when he wrote: 'When I became a man I put away childish things, including the fear of childishness and the desire to be very grown up' (Lewis 1966: 25). As I said in my introduction, when referring to Freud, all writers for children should observe the playfulness of this.

Nevertheless, as Peter Hunt reveals, Lewis's previous notion, where he said, 'I am almost inclined to set it up as a canon that a children's story which is enjoyed only by children is a bad children's story' (Lewis 1996: 24), can be summarily ignored as nonsense. Children's literature can and should be read by adults without embarrassment, that is certainly true, but I would very much regret it if children's literature became the benchmark for adult consciousness. There are many better books to be read by adults than the Narnia series, or the Harry Potter series, but far be it from me, an adult, to question a child's preference. As a critic, I can point to the problems and I can suggest alternatives, but reasons for preferment ultimately have to belong to the child (just as long as they are not being pointed at books for the wrong reasons, which is often the case). As a writer, though, it is your job to be creatively vigilant. I am not trying to stifle creativity here, but asking you to be aware of what your creativity can produce. Don't assume your great ideology is the only one and remember you are writing for the impressionable. In repeating Robert Leeson's dictum, 'You match a story to audience, as far as you can,' we can now see it is clearly an oversimplification when you also have to consider the story you are telling. As Peter Hollindale (1988: 22) writes: 'What we call "ideology" . . . is a living thing, and something we need to know as we need to know ourselves . . . because it is a part of us.' Be creatively vigilant, it is all a child reader can hope for!

This section is about fiction, then, and the writing of it. Almost every writer I have ever known (with a couple of exceptions) wants to write fiction. Why is this? If you consider it logically, it is because facts are facts (to some extent) but emotions, relationships and adventures are fluid and ever on the move. What is interesting to a child: the house or the creepy goings on inside? The field, or the mouse family living in it, whose story serves as a microcosm of real life? The helicopter hovering near by, or the stranger who is inside, following the car containing the boy who became a spy? The horse in the field, or the boy who trained it as if by magic? The mirror on the wall, or the reflection in the mirror whose eyes are a different colour? The magic flying scooter, or the flight?

There are two ways to address the issue of age groups: one is to write your story and see where it fits, and the other is to target your writing. Remember, though, what you are targeting is story as nurtured experience. In a story for teenagers I wouldn't hesitate to drop in the odd profanity, dead body, sexual innuendo and tough talk, but for age eight I would avoid all of these. And the story itself would be radically different. They are different children, they know different things and see the world from a different perspective from each other.

I am not going to give an explanation of options here. It is up to you to research your own field. However, the following story categories seem to be popular for all ages:

- Mysteries
- Adventures
- Animals
- Ghosts
- Science Fiction
- Horror
- School
- Fantasy
- Myths and legends

- History
- Humorous

But, of course, a piece of fiction can be a combination of these. Nothing complements a ghost story better than a little black humour about a dead cat that is really alive (or is it?). Once again, get to know what you want to write and research it. A friend of mine was putting her main character in a police cell but didn't even know what one looked like. Her local police station locked her up for research (in fact I think she's still there – the solitude and three square meals a day has done her writing no harm at all, even if she is beginning to look a bit like Ben Gunn). But I digress. The list above should not be considered as gospel. Trends in publishing happen like anywhere else. Find out what is currently in vogue. I 'listen in' to an Internet writing for children chatroom and the most interesting chat is almost always about writers' research.

I have already told you much about writing fiction in the previous chapters. What you need to know here is there are no boundaries, although, as I have said above, if you want to write an extremely polemical piece be prepared to have it scrutinised and rejected for that very reason. Surely the most important thing to remember is that the stories have to be good. And better than average is still not really good enough for most publishers these days.

Short fiction

Short Fiction	Running	Read to/read aloud/read alone
	Age 4–7	Picture Books – up to 1,500 words
		Series Fiction – up to 6,000 words
		Collected Short Stories – up to 1,500 words
		Television Tie-in

The parameters are fairly clear here because the 'reading age' of the child is aligned to the experience. At four children are still being read to, although they are beginning to read aloud to parents and also beginning to pick up books for reading themselves. However, by the time they are seven (and if everything is going to plan, literacy-wise) they should be able to read short novels for themselves. So there is a big ability spread here.

Read aloud books

These are short novels or collections of stories. The text, then, while still simple, like the picture book, can be slightly more sophisticated and you have a larger word count in which to tell the story. But don't let the larger word count fool you. If you merely fill it up with descriptive prose or delays that go nowhere, your story will go nowhere. Take this example:

> Joe is having a long lie in bed. He is making plans. Today is Saturday. There's no school today. Joe doesn't want to waste it by having nothing to do. He thinks he would like to go swimming. Then perhaps he could go to the cinema. That sounds like a good day. Joe stretched then yawned. 'What a good plan that is,' he said.

By the time Joe gets round to doing anything the day will be gone. You have to get him out there doing.

> 'Yes!' shouted Joe. 'It's Saturday and it is swimming day. Come on, Dad! Wake up, it's time to go!'
>
> 'Eh?' Joe's dad yawned.
>
> On school days Dad could hardly get Joe out of bed. But on Saturdays Joe can't wait to get going.

Get straight into the story without hanging around. Look, too, at the informality of the language in the text: 'Eh?' instead of 'Good morning' and 'can't' instead of 'cannot' allows for a sense of realism which children need, even when writing fantasy. You do not have to worry about being too precise with language, just as long as the grammar is essentially correct. And it is to be hoped you know the difference. The number of those who do not might surprise you. Of course, children do not always write grammatically correct prose but they have an excuse.

When writing for them you do not. Besides, a publisher will take one look at your grammatically messy manuscript then send it back!

Read aloud books are also intended to be read aloud by children. So you have to think about this in real terms. If you have never heard a five-year-old read, isn't it about time you did? Reading and vocabulary skills are in development, so too are comprehension skills (especially judgement and deduction), which are beginning to come to the fore.

Chapters

These are among the most rewarding things a new reader can ever be offered. The sense of achievement is massive, I've seen it, but the chapters have to be regulated. If, for example, you are writing a 5,000-word piece, you must consider chapter length. Keep them short and consistent. You do not want to write a 2,000-word first chapter then four short ones. Split the book evenly: 5,000 words fits ten chapters quite nicely, for example, although you would probably get away with seven or eight. There are no rules here. It is just common sense.

Does your book look like a book when you come to present it?

It is also very important to keep the story moving forward at all times when writing for this level, and short chapters help here. If the story dallies at all you will lose your listener/reader. And the high points of the narrative must be strategically placed. Cliff-hanger chapter endings and lots of 'suddenlies' suddenly seem to appear. Try to imagine each chapter like a scene in a film. If it has no conflict in it, it probably shouldn't be there. Also, there has to be a sense that something is coming next for the story to retain the attention of the child. But that something has to be worth waiting on so make sure you, at least, know what it is.

Dialogue

Dialogue is *very* important to the text, too. Children are looking to articulate the world they see and this kind of articulation is a cognitive skill they have to learn. Thus, dialogue is good to read and write, but be careful on the word usage and language. Also, think about settings. A child lives in real time, so at this age it is best to make things real, even if they are dinosaurs. Choose your plot with a sense of familiarity. Even the remarkably popular Pokémon has plots, which represent a kind of realism.

Viewpoint

This is crucial. First person and third person limited are the recommended viewpoints for this age group. First person is often ignored for the wrong reasons, and in skilled hands (like Tony Bradman with the Dilly series) it can be very refreshing for a child to read out loud. Dilly is not popular because he's cute. The series is popular because it is very well written.

Plot

Your story has to have a beginning, middle and end, and while the plot is simplified to provide only a faint subplot the texture of the story can be slightly stronger than that of a picture book. But remember, there are a number of issues you need to consider when mapping out your plot. For example:

- Is your story paced correctly? You must keep the story going. Don't write around it or get distracted or indulgent. Keep it moving forward!
- Are the next pages worth turning? After a bright opening, if your story has already started to sag in the middle are you sure you are writing the story you intend? All of us are guilty of writing into the story when we should be leading it along and this is where your plot structure comes in handy.
- Is the number of characters getting confusing? Do you need them all? Are they all moving the story forward? If not, should they be there at all? All too often odd characters with bit parts can be intrusive.
- Are you showing or telling the story? The show-not-tell problem is ever in evidence.

On the last of these points, here are two examples (the first telling; the second showing).

Tommy wasn't very well. Mum made him stay in bed. It was still only morning but Tommy was bored already. He had read all his comics and played with his Gameboy. Now there was nothing left to do.

'But why do I have to stay in bed?' asked Tommy.

'The doctor said you are to get plenty of rest,' replied Mum.

'But I feel much better. I really do,' said Tommy. 'Besides, it's boring being in bed all day. Can't I just get up for a little while?' Tommy pulled the duvet over himself, although he was already warm.

Mum frowned at Tommy. 'How can you be bored? I bought you some new comics and gave you your Gameboy.'

'That's just it,' he replied. 'I've read my comics and the Gameboy is getting boring.'

Suddenly, from under the duvet Tommy spotted something very strange going on in the garden.

The difference is palpable and, I hope you will agree, infinitely better. The rule of thumb here is simple: show not tell and keep the story going forward. If the story stands still, even for a moment, you need to make a cut. Be brutal, it's only a bunch of words, and you will write others. And if the ones you cut are any good they might be useful elsewhere.

Something else you might have noticed here is the way the dialogue is broken up. It is short and sharp and to the point. You need it to be because the story is beginning to take shape from this early set-up.

Also, while we are at it, you might like to consider the issue of 'branching'. This is a way of describing the complexity of sentences. In left-branching sentences the information comes before the verb or main noun and in right branching it comes after.[22] For example, above I wrote, 'Tommy pulled the duvet over himself, although he was already warm.' This is right branching, which is generally thought to be easier for children to understand. Left-branched, this would have read, 'Although he was already warm, Tommy pulled the duvet over himself.' This is useful to know if you ever write for educational publishers at this lower age range.

Further, while this story is not a picture book, as such, there will be some illustrations – mostly black-and-white line illustrations, as they are called. These are there to help the child understand the text and make the transition from picture books. However, unlike those in picture books, the pictures are no substitute for narrative.

Once again, do not assume you know what children need and want. I recently read a set of publisher's 'guidelines' for would-be writers for children. They were quite explicit when they said: 'We are unlikely to be interested in characters based on familiar objects or settings . . . Sandra the Squirrel, Molly the Mop, Dusty the Bin . . . the Supermarket Trolly Family always go back.' For some reason, the notion that these ideas sit well with this age group still persists. Try not to think of children's literature as *childish*. We are all capable of being represented as childish, that is a different matter, but the literature itself is mature writing for children.

On the subject of 'guidance', the most telling note is still this one which came from an international publisher: *'Please be critical of your work – is it really good enough?'* Research it and research it and research it. Every author I talk to (regardless of who they are writing for) is a skilled researcher.

Longer fiction

Longer Fiction	Racing Age 6–9	**Read alone** Short Stories – 2000+ words Short Novels – 12,000–20,000 words Series Fiction Collected Stories Television Tie-in
	Dodging Age 8–11	**Read alone** Novels – 20,000–30,000 words Series Fiction
	Trekking Age 10–12	**Read alone** Pre-teen Novels – 30,000–40,000 words Series Fiction

Flying

Age 12+   Teenage Fiction – 40,000 words and
               counting

The biggest problem you are likely to come across here is in understanding the needs of each experiential grouping. Once again the buzzword is research. The only difference is the complexity of story, language and topic, which you will have to gauge for yourself, through your research. As you can see from the word counts and so on, the boundaries are almost limitless. The same goes for the writing. Fresh and exciting ideas are called for here. The problem is in getting the idea developed. Having already decided to write in this almost limitless field (bearing mind what I said in the critical introduction to this fiction section), perhaps it is time we began to look at some of the important storytelling processes.

The biggest things to avoid in writing for this age are the everyday commonplace aspects of life. Yet, even the smallest spark can light up a story. It doesn't have to be a grand design, just don't make it plain old ordinary. Take this show-and-tell example. What I have constructed here is a very simple story about a boy who loves sport but isn't very good at it, using 'tell' first, then 'show'.

> Tom, age fourteen and nearing six feet tall, with an athletic build, was very interested in sport. Not being good at it, though, was a bit of a problem. Now he never gets the chance to improve.

> 'What age are you, Tom? Thirteen? Fourteen?'
> 'Fourteen, sir,' said Tom, shyly.
> The gym teacher looked him up and down again. 'You're built like an athlete. So why aren't you one?'
> Tom had heard that question before and the answer was always one he didn't want to give. He said nothing.
> 'Do you want to be an athlete?' asked the gym teacher.
> Tom did, more than anything in the world. 'Yeah!' he said. This was the first time anyone had asked that question. Most people just despaired.
> 'Then my job is to help you.'
> Tom was smiling so much he felt light-headed.

If Tom has been treated like a sickly dullard with two left feet all his life he (and the reader) is now about to see a change. His life is about to change and it's easy to see a classic ugly-duckling-into-swan story taking shape. What is needed in writing for this middle fiction group is the challenge of life itself. This can come at any angle, from realism, fantasy, sci-fi, humour, every storytelling process through to near non-fiction. (I despair at the word faction which is often used in these circumstances and you should, too. It is a lazy journalistic term that has no valid etymology apart from convenience.) Let's consider some of the issues, because even when we despair at the critical description of what goes on in fiction, it really is very simple. Bruno Bettelheim wrote:

> Since ancient times the near-impenetrable forest in which we get lost has symbolised the dark, hidden, near-impenetrable world of our unconscious . . . In his dark forest the fairy-tale hero often encounters the creation of our wishes and anxieties – the witch – who would not have the power of the witch . . . and use it to satisfy all his desires, to give him all the good things he wishes for himself . . . ? And who does not fear such powers if some other possesses them and might use them against him?
>
> (Bettelheim 1976: 94)

Think about it! Is this not the essence of a good novel for children? The empowering or fight against the abuse of power. Think of the forest as just a metaphor for what lurks in the great storyroom. And then consider the possibilities. This metaphorical forest can be anything we like. For example, in Robert Louis Stevenson's *Treasure Island* we are drawn to the inciting incident in Chapter 4, called 'The Sea Chest'. After the sea captain dies, Jim is looking for the key:

> 'Perhaps it's round his neck,' suggested my mother.
>
> Overcoming a strong repugnance, I tore open his shirt at the neck, and there, sure enough, hanging to a bit of tarry string, which I cut with his own gully, we found the key.
>
> (Stevenson 1987: 27)

The key unlocks the entire *Treasure Island* story, metaphorically leading to the forest of adventure. The key reveals the path to empowerment

...ches – although an abuse of power awaits its delivery. And what
...ay to deliver the key – prior to its discovery we hear of Old Flint's
...rew from the *Admiral Benbow*, the captain, Master Billy Bones the
buccaneer, Black Dog, the black spot, Blind Pew, dead man's debts,
threats of death and cutlasses and, of course, death itself.

Freud helps us to understand what it is about even the gory that
keeps us reading and writing on. It is the knowledge of the forest, the
knowledge of what scares and excites us at the same time. It is confront-
ing the previously unknown knowledge. As I explained earlier, a story
turns on conflict and inciting incident, which lead the cause and effect
onwards to where other conflicts await. After Jim finds the key, his life
is about to change for ever and it still has some way to go in the story.
Freud refers to this conflict provision in his essay, 'The Uncanny' (Freud
1990: 335–76), when he also discussess the German word *Unheimlich*.
Freud says the *Unheimlich* (literally, the unhomely) is not the opposite
of homely but that which is hidden and repressed. We accept and cope
with everyday events and conventions as homely but we repress the
Unheimlich, unhomely, potential problems. Yet, it is the *Unheimlich* that
promotes change in a novel. A mild example could be something
like, few of us would get out of the house in the morning if we thought
we would be confronted by trouble, violence. The possibility exists
but we repress and suppress it in order to get on with life. Of course, the
level of repression is graded internally, and since this is not a psycho-
analytical treatise there is little point in me giving anything but an
example here. When you are writing, though, think of the things we
all repress. It is both a pleasure and a terror principle. For the most part,
extreme emotions and events have to be contained in the everyday
scheme of life, but in novels they are the catalysts that drive the stories
forward.

We know what frightens and excites us, and it can be the same thing
or something entirely different. Like a child, I am not scared of heights,
I like being high up, but I am scared of hurting myself in the fall, for
example. So if I were to take my character to the edge of a cliff I have
a pretty good idea what could happen next and so, too, will the child
reader. Will he fall, will he be pushed?

Jacqueline Rose referred to this process when she wrote that
'children's fiction sets up the child as an outsider to its own process,

and that aims, unashamedly, to take the child in' (Rose 1994: 2). But still we read on to find out what is taking us in. Therein lies the basis of the cliff-hanger effect of children's fiction. Yet, even as children, it is the knowable that is exciting, stimulating, interesting or even scary, not the unknown, which by definition we can't know anything about. An introduction to the unknown makes it knowable and therefore an experience, but I find it difficult to accept the notion that the implied reader being taken in is unknowingly gullible and therefore more easily fooled. On the contrary, it is the author's knowledge of the implied reader which allows him or her to address that reader. A scary or exciting story for a child is only scary or exciting at the limits of its knowledge. But writers know this. What a child doesn't know or doesn't hear about he or she can't challenge or feel scared about, for example. But neither does the child learn unless such experiences are confronted – and God forbid all experiences have to be experienced, as opposed to represented in the novel. Thus, even the 'lived-out' experience provided in a story is valid. As Freud (1990: 372) says: 'The uncanny as it is depicted in *literature* . . . is a much more fertile province than the uncanny in real life, for it contains the whole of the latter and something more besides, something that cannot be found in real life.' You, as a writer, will be writing 'lived-out' experience for the child reader. It is the 'something that cannot be found in real life', which is lifelike, nevertheless. You will be taking the reader to the very edge of their experience and asking them to look over into the unknown, so that it can become known.

So write the fantastic, the extraordinary, the exciting, the interesting, the sparkling, stimulating, enticing, intimate, unfamiliar story. Take your story (and your reader) for a walk through a world in which presuppositions and assumptions about the world in which we live are challenged; cunningly and ingeniously avoid giving the whole story away before it is ready; let the reader know you are about to give them an experience never before attempted; trick and tease them; then, when you have led us all a merry dance through the magic of your narrative prose, surprise us with the subtlety, tenderness, fragility, delicacy and treat of your ending.

Virtually this entire book has been leading you to writing in this area. Go back and look at Chapter 1 again. The ideas on story, character, viewpoint, plot and dialogue are all relevant here. In addition there are some clues, hints and tips for each age range.

Racing	**Read alone**
Age 6–9	Short Stories – 2000+ words
	Short Novels – 12,000–20,000 words
	Series Fiction
	Collected Stories
	Television Tie-in

Your average child is beginning to move away from the read to/read alone type book and tackling something a little larger. It's still a *big story* but told *bigger* than picture-book length, with vocabulary and syntax that are not too taxing for beginner readers.

Generally these are sustained, linear stories with a definite storyline, the smallest of subplotting and usually a *big* premise – such as a quest, curing fear, getting away from bullies, solving a mystery. The premise is all-important. These are no longer little children but people who understand issues, right and wrong, history, time, space and a great deal more. Also, they are beginning to know what they like: ballet, football, humour, horses, bikes, adventures, holidays, action, change and so on. Search the bookshop lists once again, not to write a parody or pastiche but to see what children like. What recurs in the shops is not adult critically aware choice but what children like to buy, have bought for them or like to read.

Short novels can vary in complexity, subject matter and, of course, language. This is easy to research and a visit to a large bookshop will provide a wealth of material. In the main publishers are looking for innovative stories, page-turners about an exciting, imaginative world that compel a reader to read until the very last page, written with a strong, imaginative and original new voice. Never try to imitate someone else; it will never work.

If you hear of any advice that says something like, 'Pony stories, science fiction and fantasy stories about falling into parallel worlds are no longer fashionable,' try to ignore them and focus on what you want to write, for whom and what you want to say. There is always an exception for a well-told, well-written story. After all, who would have thought a sub-Gothic school story about wizards (so old fashioned) would take the world by storm? Of course, Harry Potter did just that because it is a good story, well told.

And so now we come to the Harry Potter generation.

Dodging   **Read alone**
Age 8–11   Novels – 20,000–30,000 words
                        Series Fiction

Trekking   **Read alone**
Age 10–12   Pre-teen Novels – 30,000–40,000 words
                        Series Fiction

As you can see, I have split the eight to thirteen age grouping into two. This age grouping travels the length and breadth of childhood, through puberty and even beyond, for some, into early adulthood. There is little they will not have heard of and perhaps even witnessed first hand by the time they have left children's books altogether.

Nevertheless, through stories there is much you as a writer can do to assist in developing the world you will be representing. All publishers are looking for the same things in fiction for this level. It's not so much original themes, which are almost impossible to find, but original approaches and viewpoints to accompany strong, original stories.

The complexity of plot and language need to address the age/experience range: never write at the reader or down to them, but for them. If the novel does not greet the reader on equal terms it has already failed. Nor should you make assumptions about what children want. Scatological humour (for example) is not gendered but it does have its limits when writing about serious issues, like girls and boys, growing up, abuse, bullying, sex, drugs and rock and roll, smoking, illness, race, same-sex romance, scoring goals, running, swimming, dancing, conservation, global warming, thieving, organ transplants, love, loss, ghosts, ghouls and broken rules.

Also, get to know what the different ages need in terms of experience, subject matter, gender difference, racial and cultural diversity. If you think I have been overplaying the 'write the height' issues, take a word from Celia Rees:

When I'm writing I don't have a certain ideal reader in mind. Partly because I want to be read by either gender with the same amount of enjoyment. Though I have to be conscious of age, because that will determine the language I use, my sentence structures and the complexity of my narrative. There is no point in writing in an elliptical manner for 8–9 year olds, because they won't be able to read it or won't want to read it. With my new six-part *H.A.U.N.T.S.* series – aimed at 8–12 year olds – I've had to be disciplined and to simplify the way I write.

(Rees, in Carter 1999: 202)

This whole piece is well worth a read because Celia Rees does what most writers can't do: she explains some of the processes she uses when writing and they are credible. I recommend you read it if you get the chance.

Teen fiction

Flying	**Read Alone**
Age 12+	Teenage Fiction – 40,000 words and counting

I called this section 'Flying' because out of all the age groups this is the most difficult to pin down. What is a teenager, after all? A young adult; a new adult; an old child? Teen fiction is one of the most fraught and, at the same time, exciting points on the writing for children scale, mainly because these children are not conventionally childlike, sitting as they do on the cusp of the grown-up world. You are likely to get a thirteen-year-old girl reading Joanne Harris's *Chocolat* and a fourteen-year-old boy reading Irvine Welsh's *Trainspotting* or vice versa, while a great many of your potential readers will also be studying texts like Shakespeare's *Macbeth*, Austen's *Pride and Prejudice* and Melville's *Moby Dick*, rather than reading the latest Point Horror from Scholastic, although that too has its attractions. We need to consider this area carefully because many of the things I have said above about children do not refer to *these* children, while others do. Teenage years are paradoxical, confusing, curious, extremely interesting, depressing, fascinating, sad, happy and every other invective, subjective and objective term that can be coined.

In the UK alone it is said that some 130,000 teenagers or near teenagers run away from home every year. This is an extraordinary statistic, but couched in it is a litany of causes from sex abuse to a spirit of adventure. Under eighteen years of age, these are people without certain rights: they have no voting power, no bargaining powers (apart from labour and sex) and all too easily, at this extreme end, teenagers can become a forgotten class who survive through begging, stealing or prostitution, and indeed many are sexually abused on the streets. Writing teenage fiction has a wide brief and, while graphic does not have to be explicit, the stories have to be real, even if fantasy. They have to be able to deal with everything life throws at them with a sense of purpose. Futile nihilism may sit well with Gothic rock or Kurt Cobain acolytes but to what extent it should figure in teen fiction is a question of responsibility.

Young adults (for that is what the early teens most certainly are, especially when we realise that childhood, as a legally defined term, is not much older than the last century) are now conscious of, and trying to make greater sense of, their own and other people's personalities. As Nicholas Tucker (1991: 145–6) writes:

> At whatever level of complexity, however, stories for the eleven to fourteen age-group usually reflect their audience's increasing pre-occupation with the need to acquire a consistent sense of identity . . . readers are now chiefly interested in more adult-seeming behaviour.

To this end, they are beginning to understand the world in more abstract terms, where metaphor and metonym, relationship and simile take on a new resonance, along with adult realities.

Furthermore, what we are also dealing with in this age group is an emotional and physical time-bomb ticking away. The pre-pubescent, pubescent and post-pubescent adolescents rub shoulders in a frictional world at which fiction can only gasp. Writing for them is a challenge. Are you ready for it? You should be, you have been there. There is no point in going into denial, like an early teenager.

One of the best pieces of advice I ever read on the subject of teenage fiction was written by Adele Geras and appeared in the magazine on children's books *Books for Keeps*. Geras (in Powling 1994: 193–4) wrote:

> I have one word of warning for writers of stories for teenagers: *beware of being too trendy and up-to-date*. Nothing has less street-cred than yesterday's slang, and you may find yourself hoist with your own petard if you try to be up-to-the-minute in the matter of pop-groups and so on . . . do your own thing. It's better than putting on a fancy dress of grooviness which any teenager will see through instantly.

We can add to this. Do you know who the reader is? Do you know anything about teenage culture? Only last week I mentioned the Sex Pistols to my current crop of undergraduate students. 'Who?' came the response. 'Oh well,' I replied, feeling my age. The point is to try to be aware of teen culture, read their magazines, talk to them, but never try to be them. You will fail. Don't try to keep up with transient trends, fashions, etc. By the time your book is written and on the shelf they have already moved on.

Most importantly, remember that teenage readers are mature readers who know what and who they like. Do you know what that is, though? Frankly, what you find offensive (or gross) they probably will too. But we can all give and take offence. Young adults are just a microcosm for the whole of society: they can range from the disaffected to the wittiest, most intelligent people I have ever met – and these two elements are not always dissociated. For all their sex, drugs and rock and roll reputation, they are erudite, well read, computer and Internet literate, and tuned-in to world events, major issues and opinions. Do not underestimate them.

There has been a big change in the teen fiction market in the last ten years or so. It is an area ripe for good writing. This ranges from series fiction, like Scholastic's Point series, to the one-off, well-crafted novel, such as Melvyn Burgess's *Junk* (that is not to say the series literature is not similarly well crafted – it's just more formulaic but I would never knock it). What you need to aim for is a book such a reader would read for pleasure, in their spare time, as a challenge, as a treat; in other words, for the same reasons you read. These readers are already reading prescribed books for school examinations, but they need something else. At the lower end of the age scale they may be reading writers such as Joanne Rowling, Jackie Wilson, Philip Pullman, Paula Danziger, Judy Blume and Anne Fine. Edgier writers like Robert Cormier, Aiden Chambers, Dodie Smith, Alan Garner and Melvyn Burgess begin to come into the frame as the age scale grows, as does reading maturity, and you are now sitting on the difficult cusp of the teen/adult market. If you have a great story it is a great place to be. If not, think seriously about sitting here because it is probably the toughest writing position of all.

Series fiction

Victor Watson, in the introduction to his book *Reading Series Fiction*, quotes a wonderful little anecdote from a schoolchild who said: 'starting a new novel was like going into a room full of strangers, but starting a book in a familiar series was like going into a room full of friends' (Watson 2000:). Indeed, I am sure we all feel this when we finish a good novel; we wish we could just go on and on. Once I begin, I could read Anne Tyler or J.M. Coetzee endlessly.

Series fiction has its highs and lows. I particularly admire series fiction writers such as Tony Bradman, for Dilly, Humphrey Carpenter, for Mr Majeika, Jill Murphy, for Worst Witch, Judy Waite, for Horse Healer, and there are many others. There are also many multi-authored series to be commended: Scholastic's Point series is very well written. Then, of course, there's the other side of it. It is only a personal opinion, but the heavily stylised, formulaic, *Animal Ark*, from the mythical Lucy Daniels, leaves me cold.

There are some very important rules to be considered when writing series fiction. As someone who has written thirteen novels in a series, as a television tie-in, I will give you some idea of what you need to pay attention to.

Character continuity is very important. It is for this reason that you might find it wise to create a series 'bible'. In the bible you can write down the name of each major character (i.e., each character who will have a repeating part throughout the series – this is not required for occasional bit-part players). In *Dilly the Dinosaur*, for example, Dilly, Dorla, Mother and Father are defined through specific personality traits, use of dialogue, viewpoint and so on, and these have to be maintained through each story (not as easy as it looks, I can assure you). Imagine, too, what would happen in the Mr Majeika series if Hamish Bigmore became something he is not, like nice (unless it was part of the plot). For a larger series, the bible helps you to define your characters, giving them an age, family (or not), definable traits, like scary, sporty, posh and so on. In the series of novels I wrote there were so many characters, ranging from Emperor Nero and his sidekick Snivilus Grovelus, to Ben the Baker and a collection of fictional children. The bible had already been done for the animation films and I found it extremely useful when developing the personalities of the children in the novels.

The bible, then, does not mean your characters cannot develop. They can and do, but you must be careful to make development slight. If your reader does not read the stories in sequence, for example, development can become confusing. Acquiring a new baby brother in book six when he did not exist in book two, for example, is the kind of change that could be problematic. As Victor Watson (2000: 8) reveals, 'Antonia Forest once admitted in an author's note to *The Thuggery Affair* that her characters had aged only eighteen months in a historical period of seventeen years – and that was only the sixth novel in a series of ten.'

It is in this sense that Enid Blyton gets it right by keeping the same characters in her series fiction. Joanne Rowling might find this to be problematic for the Harry Potter series; not now, as it is being written and she carries her ageing reader with her, but in the future, twenty years hence, say, because eventually it looks like the series could be read as one entire novel charting the growth of the young wizard (wizard idea, if you ask me). But the series, will need to be read in sequence if the ageing connections are to be made.

What you must never do is write a series like a soap opera. You will find that animation film series, children's television programming and series fiction, especially for the lower ages, do not sit well with having to retain prior knowledge. Each book, show or whatever has to stand alone. Especially for the early ages, five to nine, you need to be able to pick up any episode without reference to what went before. The characters may still develop, but the degree of development seen in Harry Potter would never work in *Worst Witch* by Jill Murphy or

Dilly the Dinosaur by Tony Bradman. You will find that only some of your readers/viewers would stay the course and you will definitely write yourself problems when trying to retain a soap-opera effect.

Most of this is common sense. A character shouldn't change sex between chapters, and the same goes for volumes (unless, of course, it is material to the plot – volume five, *When Betty Became Bob*, now there's an idea).

Writing series fiction can be as liberating as it is restricting, and it should not be dismissed too easily as popularism, which is nothing but a cultural construct, in any case. Jack Zipes's mistaken swipe at the Harry Potter series as popularist is itself ideologically problematic. As Watson (2000: 3) reminds us, 'the act of reading is itself a locus of complex personal and ideological pressures'. Series fiction can be as challenging as any other literature and the discerning writer knows this. Critics (like Charles Sarland (1996)) can be as sniffy as they like in criticising something like Point Horror, but if a child reads nothing but series fiction, at least the child is reading. Speaking as someone who also lectures on nineteenth-century fiction, I have read some pretty creaky so-called classics in my time. Did I mention my dislike of Thomas Hardy? And while I have problems with some series fiction, Narnia springs to mind again, it is only in relation to the panoply of better or more appropriate books available. Narnia is better than nothing at all, for nothing is surely the desert where all stories lie buried under the vast sands, only rising occasionally to shimmer at the non-reader as an unreachable mirage. If series fiction brings the mirage closer, then get serious about writing it.

The same rules apply: please try to write it well. Like all fiction, don't treat it like something you can just knock out as a little cash cow while the magnum opus is brewing. To repeat what I said in the introduction, all readers, children included, should have the quality of writing they deserve. It is entirely appropriate that we give them the best we have. Writers cannot assume they are giving children what they want without knowing what they need.

As Italo Calvino once wrote (1986: 88): 'Literature is not school. Literature must presuppose a public that is more cultured, and *more cultured than the writer himself*. Whether or not such a public exists is unimportant.' Series fiction writers need not assume their reader is an inferior beast with no appetite for the books they read. A look at the adult bestseller lists reveals the subjectivity of reading choice does not necessarily have anything to do with quality, and I am sure we can all point to some pretty poor books. But you should at least begin by writing the best you have to offer.

Submission

Before I leave this section I feel I should address the submission of fiction to a publisher. Publishers are not some alien culture. Nor are they gods, demagogues, angels or devils in disguise. They are people who publish books and make a living out of doing so. To them it is a job. Vocationally, perhaps, it might also be a pleasure, but it is their business and all of them are looking for the next good thing. They are judged on their successes and their success relies on you, the writer.

When submitting to a publisher you must remember a number of courtesies: be polite in your very short letter, which tells them about you and your book; send a tidy, well-cared-for text – no one likes to read a smelly book (you would be surprised how many people don't seem to know this: opening an envelope smelling of cigarette smoke, oven chips and stained with jam may reveal the next international bestseller but give yourself a break and try to send it clean and tidy).

If it is a novel you must set it out like one. Indent paragraphs and make sure it is double-spaced and typed in a readable font – Times New Roman, 12 point, is an ideal presentation typeface for those of you using computers. Remember, the publisher reads a great many manuscripts; don't try to cram all of your text on to as few pages as possible. Of course, you must always type/print on one side of the paper only; double-sided text in draft or presentation form is a right pain for any reader. Provide a plain and simple title page and keep the presentation simple. Don't try to replicate a book, or indeed the proofs, that is not your job, and tying your masterpiece up in little ribbons may look cute but it gets no points.

Be businesslike. When submitting, you should send a full and extensive synopsis and two or three sample chapters (which need not run in sequence, although it is usually best to send the first chapter), but you should not do this until you have written the whole manuscript.

You can send the whole manuscript if you wish – although those of you practised in this and the art of rejection know how much it costs to send and receive it back, in your own stamped addressed envelope. It soon mounts up. Only experienced writers can get away with sending all they have for a commission.

If a publisher shows an interest, you need to follow through quickly or the opportunity can be missed. There is no point in sending an idea that *might* be finished next year. Publishers move on, get pregnant, leave, become distracted by something else and so on. If they say they like your work, get on to it and them right away. Believe me, the shine soon goes when delays occur. But do not pester the publisher. Things get done in their own time. I know of one publisher who paid another to take an author off his hands because he pestered him so much.

Once you have submitted get on with the next project, because the submitted one can take up to six months to elicit a response (often likely to be *no* or *sorry*, anyway, and you must be ready for this, because it happens to us all). Another thing to remember is that if you are submitting to educational publishers you must expect the time scales to be even longer. They not only consider publishing but road test the material for suitability. Even after writing, rewriting, redrafting and the commissioning of illustrations the whole thing can be cancelled at the last minute.

The synopsis shouldn't be as difficult as maybe you fear. Think of it as the packaging of an Easter egg. Even if it is just plain old chocolate inside it has to attract your attention in the first place. So don't try to summarise your story; instead, talk it up, dress it up in all its finery and then fly it like a kite for all to gaze and wonder at. This looking but not touching stage is the point where the recipient publisher decides he or she can't wait to reel it in to read. If they are disappointed, well that's your fault for not doing a good enough job, I'm afraid. At the point of synopsis, you are the only person who knows if it is any good or not – if it is good, persuade everyone else!

I hope I have covered everything you need to know. All that remains for me to say to you potential novelists is good luck, you will need it, we all do, but get to know your craft. Then craft your story well. Luck is only a small part of the equation.

4 Write the rest

The title for this chapter seemed like a good idea at first. The initial plan was to address and include material on non-fiction, poetry and film and new media. It was only when I came to research it that I realised the difficulties. The sections I had planned on poetry, film and new media could be whole books on their own. I will give some introductory material, which should help you to make a start, but this can only scratch the surface because film and new media is becoming such a vast area so quickly that I think the proposed book will have to precipitate a major change in current print publishing. If the rumours I hear are true, educational publishing is about to change in a very dramatic way, and the Internet and computers with video coupling, digitally enhanced film footage, animatics, animation, hotspots and links will have huge parts to play in this. But this revolution is in its infancy, and even with new technology looming publishers will still need talented writers. *Poetry* for children, too though, needs a serious re-addressing and I will introduce some of the issues, which are bigger than my ability to fix.

Non-fiction

Non-fiction is an odd concept, especially when we think of what it contains. Taken literally, it refers to writing that is not fictional. Yet, if we consider it carefully, the dividing line between fiction and non-fiction is very slim. As Margaret Meek (1988: 8) says,

The simplified formulation of this division is in the labels 'fiction' and 'non-fiction'. The latter are thought of as books offering readers representations of the 'actual' world from which that world can be learned about. The former is the category of stories, novels, which are for pleasure, recreational reading and informal learning.

Yet what is non-fiction? History, biography, poetry, religion, science, sport, nature, geography, humour, jokes, verse, even songs: it is a mixed bag which also finds its way into fictional writing. Indeed, this non-fiction book I am writing for you contains much fiction (some might say it is all fiction – that was a joke, by the way, which is another non-fiction topic). Perhaps it might be more relevant to suggest that non-fiction recreates a view of a world which is occupied by human curiosity.

Generally speaking, writing non-fiction is not like writing a novel. You would not lock yourself away in a garret preparing your magnum opus in secret until you are ready to unleash it on the world. You would look for a commission first. Before I began this book I spoke to Routledge about it. I presented them with an idea and then after an editorial discussion and peer assessment of the proposal they commissioned me to write it. What I did prior to this, though, was to consider whether there was a need and an opening.

The first question I had to ask myself was simply this: is there a need for a *Write for Children* book? My answer was based on my own research. I run Writing for Children, currently the only Master's degree course in the world to concentrate specifically on creative writing for children, and I felt I needed a text specifically suitable for use on the course. No such text existed. This also meant that other courses didn't have access to such a book either. So I decided to write it. Of course, there are a number of How to Write for Children books which do some of the basic work, but I needed something with a little more depth to it, hence this book you are reading.

The proposal was simple. I outlined in three or four pages what I intended to write, giving a brief breakdown of chapters, targeted audience and potential market. Having identified these, Routledge agreed the possibilities were appropriate to them as publishers and the commission went ahead. It is the same when writing non-fiction *for* children.

Why I chose Routledge as my publisher may be another question. The answer is simple: Routledge have the kind of profile and book list that could support a book like this. They are respected university/ education publishers and the book does not look out of place alongside others on their list. This kind of choice is very important. Recently I published a non-fiction book with Paternoster Press, but since they are primarily religious publishers this book is not appropriate for them or their list. You need to check this kind of information. If you have an idea, who do you see being interested in it and why?

Before you approach a publisher, look very carefully at your idea. There is no point in giving children what you think they want without knowing what they need, and this has to be a priority.

What do any of us need from non-fiction? A list of facts or even a whole book comprising non-fiction material is simply of no use to the average person unless it contributes to their wider picture of the world and experience. Knowing the theory of relativity makes no sense unless it has a context into which it can be usefully placed. Our reading skills and understanding of meaning are enhanced by the factual information we receive from any text, but the non-fiction text is only a supplement to our wider understanding.

It must also be acknowledged that many non-fiction books are the product of teamwork, when a publisher will bring a production team together. Rarely have I seen great examples of these, although with new print and computer compositing and scanning techniques they are getting better. The trouble is they always seem so boringly put together: books on India written by people who have never been there; or books supposedly written by a child of a particular culture who speaks like a university-educated adult (and I know you have seen these, too). Part of the problem is that the books may look good but the text is usually awful and there really is no excuse for this.[23]

What you will find is that virtually every subject you come to attempt will already have been tackled. The secret is to come up with a new angle, a new way of telling the story, coming at the story of the fact from a new, exciting and interesting direction. This is where your fictional and storytelling skills will come into play.

While second person may seem the most natural viewpoint for non-fiction (see 'Viewpoint' section in Chapter 2), it can also be dry as dust if not handled carefully. If you have ever read the instructions for your washing-machine you will know what I mean. You can change the Dr Dryasdust approach, though, by altering the way you approach the provision of information. In this book, for example, I have occasionally adopted a first-person narrative, which conveys what 'I' want to say to 'you', the second person. Rather than just giving a set of instructions, I present the information as shared practice. This allows me to take a more informal approach to the information without losing my authority over it, and this can be very effective indeed. That is not to say you can wax overlyrical about the information you are trying to convey (as I have been guilty of – such is the nature of writing about writing), but think in the same terms as a picture book. Tell a big story small, or at least smaller, making sure the information is not buried in the rhetoric.

Some of the best non-fiction books I have seen recently have been written and illustrated by Helen Cowcher. She manages to weave a story so finely through a factual text that it has the same qualities as a very good picture book, and I recommend you look at her work. But she is not alone in this. What I am saying is non-fiction should not be a dreary reproduction of facts. We have come a long way since Walter Scott coined the name Dr Dryasdust for his academic historian in *The Heart of Mid-Lothian*. As writers such as Terry Deary and Diana Kimpton have clearly shown, non-fiction can be seriously good fun. The best advice I have ever received on this came from a non-fiction commissioning editor when he said that the problem with non-fiction is that most of it consists of 'passionless, anonymous texts'.[24] It needn't, though.

While Margaret Mallett (1992: 50) has a point when she says, 'a salacious and unnecessarily gory approach is not recommended – but rather an honest presentation of the different aspects of the subject', it might be suggested that Terry Deary's Horrible Histories do lean towards the gory. Indeed, it is this that keeps the child reader interested. We are all interested in the gore and the guts. Sticking to facts, without the unsavoury dressing, leads to a bland predictability that does not represent true life at all. On this issue, Eleanor von Schweinitz (in

Powling 1994: 126) has said that the writer of non-fiction is allowed personally to engage with the text:

> Some of the most lively writing can be found in books on controversial topics where publishers have been willing to tackle subjects that give rise to strong emotions and differences of view. The insistence in some quarters than an issue should be considered from all viewpoints and in a dispassionate manner is hardly a prescription for lively writing. And the dutiful drawing up of a balance sheet is unlikely to provoke interest, let alone thought, on the part of the reader.

What Deary does is put the life, the excitement back into history. His quick quizzes, variable narratives, test your teacher sections and general dip-in approach make locating history enjoyable. Yet, one should never think the histories are not well researched; they are, and the books are real history books.

Do not make the mistake of thinking that non-fiction is about facts by ignoring this simple point: *Facts are about people!*

The very term factual writing is fraught with difficulty. But non-fiction is all about us and the way we function, live in time, history, culture, project the future, drive cars, freeze food, cook . . . the list is endless. We live in a world in which we have to function, where the creativity has to be counterbalanced by a sense of practicality. Before typing this book I had to learn some facts, about using computers, for example. A whole pile of factual information has gone into this writing, most of which you will never see. So think about how much children really need to know. Is your project worthy of the effort you have invested in it?

One of the ways in which I have tried to get my students to consider this issue is by asking them to consider writing by taking on a persona as Aesop's brother. The technique is simple but it tends to produce incredibly rewarding non-fictional stories. What they have to do is come up with a factual story, or something which might fall into the non-fiction genre like one of Aesop's fables, but a point in history ('I see no ships') works, too, then tell the story through a voice not normally associated with the empirical idea of a fact. For example,

Aesop's brother would tell the fable differently from Aesop. A cabin boy at the Battle of Trafalgar has a different story to tell from Dr Dryasdust's historical account. Imagine, for example, you are a boy chimney-sweep in Victorian London (with Blake's 'weep, weep' echoing in your head). You could take all the facts of that grotesque occupation, the dirt, the grime, the early deaths, the poverty, the poor sanitation (you might gather this is not *Mary Poppins*), then try to tell it as a 'true-life' story. Anyone fortunate enough to have read Alexander Solzhenitsyn's *A Day in the Life of Ivan Denisovich* might agree there is a good story for the telling there. The fictional Ivan tells us of the real trauma of a Soviet Gulag. This kind of book humanises the fact for us. The fact is contextualised and given feelings and reactions rather than being presented as a bald, disembodied lacuna. But this is not easy. As Hayden White (1978: 50) wrote:

> Only a chaste historical consciousness can truly challenge the world anew every second, for only history mediates between what is and what men think ought to be within humanising effect. But history can serve to humanise experience only if it remains sensitive to the more general world of thought *and* action from which it proceeds and to which it returns.

What is essential in non-fiction is getting the facts straight. If they are researched and in place a good narrative structure can only enhance them. When I co-created *The Storykeepers*, translating elements of the New Testament into animation film, the theological and historical information in the film was addressed with academic rigour. And as I write a new series, based on the Old Testament, that same rigour is being applied. What we did in the first series was to flesh out the New Testament narrative by telling a story of the first storytellers who, during the first hundred years after the birth of Jesus, told the stories in the oral tradition of the day. This was set in a period before the Gospels were written down and assembled into the New Testament. The success of that series was founded on the combination of fact, history, geographical location and theology with a highly appropriate storytelling technique. In terms of animation for children, *The Storykeepers* pioneered an entirely new concept in biblical storytelling, which has since gone on to be imitated elsewhere. With some fictional elements for support, who can deny the series is also non-fiction? The aim was principally to reveal the New Testament/non-fiction as a story about people before the story was written down, but within the fictional narrative we revealed the facts by stealth.

It is also appropriate to check national education requirements to see what schoolchildren need to study. When educational publishers are looking for material they are also looking to target specific requirements. Recently I have seen requests for rewritten myths and legends, for example, and this comes into a non-fiction remit. So, too, have I seen some great books on mountain biking as a sport, with some outstanding pictures. The remit is huge. How big is your imagination? If you can imagine a truly great non-fiction series, there are people out there waiting for it.

Especially relevant to educational publishing, the literacy hour in schools (certainly in the UK) has changed the demand for non-fiction to a quite staggering degree. It is now a major part of literacy in schools. So the requirements are increasingly challenging, but you need to know what the literacy demands are. The writer Diana Kimpton, who also runs the www.wordpool.co.uk website (which is all about writing for children and I recommend you visit it regularly for updates and useful information), has kindly allowed me to reproduce the following for you. The information has been distilled from papers prepared for teachers about the literacy strategy.

> First, all children, even the youngest, are taught how to use a non-fiction book properly, so even the simplest book needs a contents page and an index. Page headings and sub-headings are also important and so are captions for the illustrations. A glossary is a useful addition too and one welcomed by teachers but it's not always feasible to put one in a book with only a few lines of text.
>
> Second, non-fiction for the literacy hour is divided into categories. You will need to keep these strongly in mind when you are planning books for the educational market as teachers will want to know which one your book fits into. Publishers will want to know this too and they often use the categories as part of the brief

when commissioning work. For instance, they may ask for ideas for non-chronological reports for six-year-olds.

Here's a list of the main categories to help you understand what everyone is talking about.

Discussion texts

These look at two or more points of view on an issue. They discuss the pros and cons of each point of view and examine the evidence for them before drawing a conclusion or leaving the readers to make up their own minds. Balanced books on controversial topics like fox hunting and animal experimentation fit here but ones which are heavily biased in one direction are really persuasive texts.

Explanation texts

As the name suggests, these explain how or why something happens or answer a question. They include books with titles like *How the universe began*, *How your body works* and *What happens to the food you eat*.

Instruction texts

These tell the reader how to do something, often with the help of lists of instructions and diagrams. 'How to . . . ' books fit here, as do cookery books, art books and books on improving your football.

Persuasive texts

These aim to persuade the reader to agree with the author or to follow a particular course of action like not smoking or keeping safe in the sun. Although they may look at alternative opinions, they don't do this in the balanced way of a discussion text.

Recount texts

These retell a sequence of events in chronological order, although there is often an introductory section to set the scene. Biographies and autobiographies are recounts. So are books with titles like *A day in the life of a fireman*, *The discovery of penicillin* and *The ascent of Everest*.

Reference texts

These present a collection of short pieces of information organised in a way that makes them easy to locate – usually alphabetical. Encyclopedias, dictionaries and bird books fit in this category.

Report texts or non-chronological reports

These tackle a particular topic like cats, puppets or dinosaurs in a way that is independent of the passage of time. They often begin with a general introduction (what's a puppet?), followed by sections on different aspects of the topic (types of puppet, famous puppets, puppet theatres, etc.).

As you can see the scope is quite massive. We must go back to one of the mantras of this book: *Research!*

Research, research, research. I cannot say it often enough. You need to do it. My doctoral thesis, another piece of non-fiction, took three years to research and write. This book has been written after years of working on the subject. Yet, I also know people who want to be writers who have not visited a library in years. How can this be? I ask you to ask them.

It should also be said here that unless you have contact with educational publishers who commission such material, knowing what is required is crucial. Contact them for yourself and introduce your work to them. Publishers in the trade market do not have the same emphasis on the literacy hour, although recently I have seen they are keen to bump against it in the production of more tangential material dealing with similar subjects. Indeed, national curriculum links are popular. As Diana Kimpton (2000) has stated, 'great importance is laid on what editors refer to as the WOW factor'. Non-fiction that makes children say, 'Wow!' is always highly prized. This should be considered in your writing. Try to make the material sparkle, write with passion, eschew anonymous blandness. As an academic, I have read enough boring books on great subjects to last me a lifetime. While Kant, Hegel, Freud, Darwin, Marx, Benjamin, Foucault, Derrida *et al.* have *never* bored me, some academic material I have read, even recently while researching this book, has left me yawning (hopefully I have not had a similar effect on you). It is the writer and the writing, not the material, that are at fault here, and you must always bear this in mind. All of the writers I have named in this paragraph are addressing difficult concepts and ideas, but they write brilliantly. Having a fact to tell is not enough: you have to write readable text; you have to write it well. You have to write what your reader wants to read. They can never be forced into reading it and they need no encouragement not to read it.

Biography

Sigmund Freud once wrote: 'Anyone who writes a biography is committed to lies, concealments, hypocrisy, flattery and even hiding his own lack of understanding, for biographical truth does not exist.'[25] I have just read an autobiography (a very rare event for me) and I tend to think Freud might have been right. Nevertheless, biography for children can be extremely interesting. One of my all-time favourite children's books is Michael Foreman's *War Boy*. It has the wonderful mixture of fact and storytelling that I referred to above, but what makes it special is the way the story is told. The passion is intact and the story is kept interesting. To do this you need to know what to include and what to cut. You don't want a list of the cups of tea I drank while trying to write this chapter. Nor do you need to know how I was dressed when I wrote it (smoking jacket, cravat, silk slippers). Most biographies are full of the wrong kind of information. It is certainly a truism that half a truth can tell the bigger lie. As Albert Einstein once said, 'Not everything that can be counted counts, and not everything counts that can be counted.' The issue is that biography is as much about the biographer as the subject. It is a very subjective medium. For example, I am quite sure my account of the works of C.S. Lewis, as discussed above, would not find its way into some more reverential biographies. But this is the wont of the biographer. The objectivity is always subjective at the same time. How can it not be? Were I to write a biography on the person whose autobiography I have just read, I would have written an entirely different story – that we could see ourselves as others see us!

Crucial to biography for children is sustainable interest. We have all heard the phrase, 'I could tell the story of my life, that would be a story and a half,' yet, sad though it is to say, it probably wouldn't be a story and a half. It rarely is for anyone, which is why Freud's quotation above is so astute. Nevertheless, children are interested in people for a number of reasons. David Beckham and Jesus may make odd bedfellows (apart from in the schoolyard joke, 'Jesus saves, but Beckham nets the rebound'), but as I write both have had recent biographies written about them and both were very successful books in their own right. The crucial factor here is choosing your subject well. Chris Powling's excellent book on Roald Dahl, written for children, is a very good example of what can be achieved when you address the kinds of question children demand answers to.

Does your biography answer the questions a child, your reader, would be interested in? Don't get carried away with your own interest in the subject, which can work to the detriment of your reader. When writing a biography, you need to get to know your subject. This is obvious, but try to get under their skin. If they are funny, for example, try to capture what makes them so. If they are brilliant or brave or just plain famous for fame's sake, try to capture them in prose. Your book is a window into their very being. The worst thing you can ever do to anyone (and yourself) is to write a turgid book. All you will do is turn everyone else off. Consider how the interesting can be rendered boring. It is hard to imagine, but you have undoubtedly read something of this ilk.

Take Einstein's advice, cut out the irrelevance and keep your biography interesting. The minute a child begins to skip pages, or, worse, puts the book down you have done your subject and the child a disservice.

Humour

In the park some children were playing on the Wishing Slide. When Sian slid down the Wishing Slide she shouted, 'Gold,' and at the bottom she landed in a pot of gold. Next it was Billy's turn. As he slid down the

Wishing Slide he shouted, 'Silver,' and at the bottom he landed in a pot of silver. Billy's cousin forgot it was the Wishing Slide. He slid down shouting, '*Weeeee!*' And landed with a splash.

Humour and children go hand in hand – they love a great laugh. My seven-year-old daughter told me that joke. Humour books, joke books and humorous histories, for example, often come into the non-fiction category, and it is a very subjective medium. Don't be fooled into thinking only the scatological is funny to children. Their understanding of a funny situation is closer to real life than zany, but that is not to say the zany is not funny to them – although, once again, this is subject to experience. Jokes involving wordplay, for example, rarely if ever work for the younger ages if they don't know the root of the joke in the first place. I once wrote a critique on a Disney film called *Detective Tigger, Private Ear* (see Melrose 2001). Even the title is problematic. A wordplay on 'private eye' can't work when the target audience (four-to seven-year-olds) doesn't know what a detective is, far less a private eye. Again, though, it is easy to overcome this problem by doing your research. I recently read *Bloody Scotland* by Terry Deary, and the humour, combined with Martin Brown's wonderful illustrations, was gloriously funny to me. However, my children (who have to live with a bloody Scotsman) just didn't get it. But not yet was the key. They are too young for the 'wirry' joke, which I nearly fell apart at (and do read it, it's very funny). But 'wirry not', my children *will* get it when the time is right and perhaps a little local colour will make it even funnier for them. I hope so.

Writing humour is a real knack. It is all about pace and timing (now where have I written that before). If you have an ear for humour and have a good book's worth of it, write a sample and an outline of the book for a suitable publisher because they are always on the lookout for something new. But make sure it works. If your friends do not think it is funny, it probably isn't. Further, does your humour transcend the captive audience of friendship? It isn't nearly as easy as it looks, said the actress to the bishop (which, of course, means nothing to a child).

That's not to say your other writing has to be devoid of humour. A good laugh can be the world's greatest tonic, and if you have a great sense of the asinine, absurd, foolish, balmy or ridiculous, polish it up and write it down.

Poetry (an introduction)

I intend to say little about poetry, and there is a very good reason for this. I believe this needs a book of its own and I am not the person to write it, although I know of a couple of very good candidates. When it comes to children's literature, poetry is probably the most seriously abused artform. For evidence of this I urge you to read Robert Hull's article 'What hope for children's poetry?' in *Books for Keeps*, January 2001. It is a review of around 100 poetry books published in 1999 and 2000 which says much more than I could even begin to in this short section.

Having just discussed biography, though, brings us to poetry quite neatly. Looking at the history of poetry, we can see that the distant Hellenic culture which produced writers such as Homer reveals poetic origins lying with the voice of the muse. The poet was merely the mouthpiece or scribe. By the end of the eighteenth century this view had radically changed, when William Wordsworth declared poetry was the expression of the self and therefore intensely biographical. As Adam Phillips (2000: 323) reveals, 'When the American poet John Ashbery was asked why his poems were so difficult he said that he noticed that if you go on talking to people they eventually lose interest, but when you start talking to yourself they want to listen in.' I find this very persuasive. Listening in to the inner thoughts, feelings and emotions of the poet seems to me to be the closest way of engaging with the writer's creativity. But this too has to be crafted, as Yeats could tell you:

> Irish poets learn your trade,
> Sing whatever is well made.

But wherefore can be found biography or any other serious subject in children's poetry, which seems to be dogged by doggerel and whimsy? In his investigation of children's poetry, Robert Hull asks whether poetry for children is morphing into crazy verse for kids? You need to consider this point and you might also consider just how much whimsical versifying the world can accept. When writing a poem, are you sure it really is one? Clearly, children like a little doggerel or whimsy every so often, but need all poetry suffer at the hands of it?

I heard a poem recently which began:

> Snaky Malaky
> jumped high off the floor,
> and swung on the handle
> and opened the door.

It has good rhythm, good sense of rhyme, and a deft touch in word choice. For example, Snaky Malaky jumps '*high* off the floor' not '*up* off the floor'. Also the poem has good movement (Snaky is in the middle of doing something) and, of course, it is simple to read and deliver. So it should be because my five-year-old son (now six) wrote it.[26] The point is this: why write like a child when the child can already do it for himself or herself. Write *for* the child, not *at* them. A good poem, like a good picture book, is a big story written differently. It is not a little verse written where any old rhyme will do. Poetry should speak of something, something big, however little it appears. It is the poet who can trace the smallest nuances of a big world. The poem has to say something about the rhythm and rhyme of life, even if it doesn't rhyme (and that can refer to discord, too).

In providing some questionable blame for what he perceives as the poetry problem in the restrictive practices of literacy hours, Robert Hull goes on to make an excellent defence of poetry which all aspiring poets should read. Perhaps this is the real rub: poetry is just not read as much as it once was and thus children are not introduced to it in the same way as they are to novels, say.

Yet, a great deal of poetry is available and being written and it needs to be worked at. Thus, what I can do here is repeat some of Hull's reading recommendations, with the addition of one of my own. This is not a canon of children's poetry but a pointer in the direction of what might be of interest to children. On this issue of a canon, when I was writing this section a review of Nobel Prizewinner Seamus Heaney's canonical new collection, *Electric Light* (Faber, 2001), appeared in the *Guardian*.[27] The reviewer wrote that the collection was 'nostalgic poetry reaching back to romanticism [*sic*]: nature, God, then ineffable, the sublime. Reliable, reassuring: yes, yes. But something more, surely, is required.' The reviewer's doubts over this collection have to be read in light of a discussion on poetry and the postmodern and no doubt many will approve of the poetry for the same reasons as the reviewer disapproves of it. But debate is healthy. Writing thrives on debate. Closure, for whatever reason, good or bad, will always end up in tyranny. Engage with the debate and the poetry then consider what you are writing.

I firmly believe that if you want to write good poetry you need to know what it reads like. There is no other way to begin and I urge you to read, read and then read some more. I read poetry almost daily. I have read the books on this list. It is the only way I can recommend you get to know what poetry for children is and perhaps even should be (although I could never force that opinion on to you). Before you write your next poem, give reading a go. Even as research it cannot be a waste of time.

Suggested reading

Poetry

- *All Sorts*, Christopher Reid
- *How to Avoid Kissing Your Parents in Public*, Lindsay MacCrae
- *In and out of the Shadows*, Sandy Brownjohn
- *Meeting Midnight*, Carol Ann Duffy
- *Never Stare at a Grizzly Bear*, Nick Toczec
- *Poems about Love*, ed. Roger McGough
- *Shades of Green*, ed. Anne Harvey
- *Stargazer*, Robert Hull
- *Talking Drums*, Veronique Tadjo
- *The Songs of Birds*, ed. Hugh Lupton
- *The World is Sweet*, Valerie Bloom
- *Werewolf Granny*, ed. Tony Bradman

Books on poetry

- *Behind the Poem*, Robert Hull
- *The Redress of Poetry*, Seamus Heaney
- *Poetry in the Making*, Ted Hughes

As you can see, there is a combination of anthologies and collections, some humorous and some not so, and books on writing poetry by poets. Happy reading!

Film and new media (an introduction)

The more I think of film and new media these days, the more daunting it becomes. As I wrote elsewhere,

> In this advanced telecommunications age of 'lived-out experience', handed to us by globalised, e-net communication; website narratives; wall to wall, terrestrial, satellite and cable-link television; video; CD-ROM; DVD; video games; holographic experience; computer-generated simulation and whatever else that lurks round the technological corner, lies the fact that the . . . televisual medium has all but replaced other forms of storytelling narrative, ask any bookseller.
>
> (Melrose 2000: 6)

There is a lot of snobbery over this. As Lisa Sainsbury has written, 'many media are overlooked by official hierarchies that tend to value the printed book over all other forms of narrative' (Sainsbury in Bearne and Watson 2000: 82). I agree, and I do not think new media necessarily must work to the detriment of reading, or writing for that matter, and as I hinted earlier it will have a huge part to play in the future of educational publishing. Indeed, much reading is necessary for new media to function at all. As Sainsbury goes on to say, 'while complementing more traditional modes of storytelling, computer games are increasingly reliant on progressive narrative structures that implicate children as readers, as much as players' (*ibid.*).

Nevertheless, I am not going to be able to address this, or indeed writing for these mediums, here. The subject is simply too large and growing to do it justice, and my plan is to write a complete follow-up book.

Here ends this book, then. I have tried to maintain a creative and critical vigilance when addressing the craft of writing for children. I hope you don't feel cheated.

Notes

Crafting and the critically creative

1 Writing for Children, King Alfred's, University College Winchester, UK
2 For story, see Melrose (2001).
3 Literacy experts, educational publishers and schoolteachers have identified the problem that it is harder to keep the *good* readers interested in reading.
4 See Hunt (1991: 155–74). The novel is called *Going Up* (McRae, 1989).
5 See Johnson (2000). See also Rob Middlehurst (2000), 'Perspectives on Narrative', *National Association for Writers in Education Journal* 2.
6 See Melrose (2001).
7 Sheppard (1999). If you log on to www.nawe.co.uk you will be able to read this article (and more) online, and I recommend you do.
8 See Melrose (2001).

Write the rights/know the wrongs

9 The quote is from Freud's essay 'The Uncanny', and it is suggested you read it in full. It will be worthwhile.
10 © Andrew Melrose, 2001.
11 I found Derrida (1978) useful on this issue.
12 The story world is the world you have created, whether it is Narnia or Echelfechin.
13 MacGuffin was a term introduced to storytelling by Alfred Hitchcock, which is an object, term or event in a story which serves as the impetus for the plot – birds in *The Birds* is a perfect example.
14 See Hunt, ed. (1999: 69–80).
15 Saboda (2000).
16 Dialogic is the word used by Mikhail Bakhtin when referring to language being Janus-faced and having a double voice, which is sensitive to the culture, language and society it comes from.

17 See Pullman in Carter (1999: 184).

Write the height

18 Ian Pillinger, *Baby Driver Books* (Peter Haddock Ltd).
19 For a balanced and unpretentious look at the debate on whether we should read Lewis or not, see Blake (2000).
20 Goldthwaite (1999) persuasively writes that Lewis's books represent a personal distortion of Christianity. Of course, this only highlights the fact that Goldthwaite disagrees with Lewis's idea of Christianity. Preferred readings of any ideology and religion are always fraught with difficulties. You must consider your own.
21 BBC Radio 4 discussion between Laurie Taylor, Jack Zipes and Nicholas Tucker on the subject of Harry Potter, 28 February 2001.
22 I got this term from Hunt (1999: 178). This is a useful book, as is the idea.

Write the rest

23 I suggest you read Robert Hull's very informative work on non-fiction. See the bibliography and especially his contribution to Prowling (1994: 133–44).
24 Thanks to Paul Harrison of Walker Books, who shared some of his wisdom with my students.
25 Freud in a letter to Arnold Zweig, 1936, refusing Zweig's request to be his biographer. See Adam Phillips (2000), *Promises, Promises*, Faber & Faber, p. 72.
26 'Snaky Malaky', by Daniel Melrose, 2001. Since it is not entirely inappropriate to the premise of this book, I have a story to tell you. When my son met the poet Robert Hull they had a short conversation which went something like this:
    'So, you're five, Daniel? When were you five?'
    'On my birthday!' replied Daniel.
27 Robert Potts, 'The View from Olympia', *Guardian*, 7 April 2001.

Bibliography

This list is split into three categories for easier access.

Some useful critical books on children's literature and storytelling

Appleyard, J.A. (1991) *Becoming a Reader: The Experience of Fiction from Childhood to Adulthood*, Cambridge University Press

Bearne, Eve and Watson, Victor (eds) (2000) *Where Texts and Children Meet*, Routledge

Bettelheim, Bruno (1976) *The Uses of Enchantment: The Meaning and Importance of Fairy Tales*, Knopf

Blake, Andrew (2000) 'Of More than Academic Interest: C.S. Lewis and the Golden Age', in M. Carretero-Gonzalez and E. Hidalgo Tenorio (eds), *Behind the Veil of Familiarity: C.S. Lewis (1898–1998)*, Peter Lang

Carpenter, Humphrey (1985) *Secret Gardens: The Golden Age of Children's Literature*, Allen & Unwin

Carpenter, Humphrey and Prichard, Mari (1984) *The Oxford Companion to Children's Literature*, Oxford University Press

Chambers, Aiden (1982) *Plays for Young People to Read and Perform*, Thimble Press

—— (1993) *Tell Me: Children, Reading and Talk*, Thimble Press

Chambers, Nancy (ed.) (1980) *The Signal Approach to Children's Books*, Kestral/Penguin Books

De Bono, Edward (1972) *Children Solve Problems*, Allen Lane

Goldthwaite, John (1996) *The Natural History of Make-Believe*, Oxford University Press

Hollindale, Peter (1988) *Ideology and the Children's Book*, Thimble Press

—— (1997) *Signs of Childness in Children's Books*, Thimble Press

Hourihan, Marjorie (1997) *Deconstructing the Hero*, Routledge

Hunt, Peter (ed.) (1990) *Children's Literature: The Development of Criticism*, Routledge

—— (1999) *Understanding Children's Literature*, Routledge

—— (2001) *Children's Literature*, Blackwell

Inglis, Fred (1981) *The Promise of Happiness, Value and Meaning in Children's Fiction*, Cambridge University Press

Mallet, Margaret (1992) *Making Facts Matter*, Paul Chapman

Meek, M. (1988) *How Texts Teach What Readers Learn*, Thimble Press

Melrose, Andrew (2000) 'Story in the Age of Electronic Reproduction', *Journal of NAWE*, 2 (http://www.nawe.co.uk)

—— (2001) *Storykeeping: the Story, the Child and the Word*, Paternoster

Melrose, A. and Brown, B. (1996) *The Storykeepers Video Series*, Paternoster

—— (1998a) *Victory*, Cassell

Nodelman, Perry (1988) *Words about Pictures*, University of Georgia Press

Powling, Chris (ed.) (1994) *The Best of Books for Keeps*, Bodley Head

Rose, Jacqueline (1994, revised edn) *The Case of Peter Pan or the Impossibility of Children's Fiction*, Macmillan

Rosen, Michael (1997) 'A Materialist and Intertextual Examination of the Process of Writing a Work of Children's Literature', Ph.D. thesis, University of North London

Sarland, Charles (1996) 'Revenge of the Teenage Horrors', in Morag Styles, Eve Byrne and Victor Watson (eds), *Voices Off Contexts and Readers*, Cassell

Tucker, Nicholas (1991 [1981]) *The Child and the Book*, Cambridge University Press

Watson, Victor (2000) *Reading Series Fiction*, Routledge

Whitehead, Winifred (1988) *Different Faces: Growing up with Books in a Multicultural Society*, Pluto Press

Zipes, Jack (1993) *The Trials and Tribulations of Little Red Riding Hood*, Routledge

—— (1995) *Creative Storytelling – Building Community, Changing Lives*, Routledge

—— (1997) *Happily Ever After – Fairy Tales, Children and the Culture Industry*, Routledge

Some useful works on critical and creative writing

Abbs, Peter (1996) *The Polemics of Imagination*, Skoob Books

Auden, W.H. (1963) *The Dyer's Hand, and Other Essays*, Faber & Faber

Bakhtin, M.M. (1986) *Speech Genres and Other Late Essays*, University of Texas Press

Benjamin, W. (1992) *Illuminations*, ed. H. Arendt, Fontana

Booth, W. (1983) *The Rhetoric of Fiction*, University of Chicago Press (Penguin reprint, 1991)

Boud, D. (1995) *Enhancing Learning through Self-assessment*, Kogan Page

Bradbury, M. (ed.) (1990) *The Novel Today: Contemporary Writers on Modern Fiction*, Fontana

Carter, James (ed.) (1999) *Talking Books*, Routledge

Carter, R.A. (1997) *Investigating English Discourse: Language, Literacy and Literature*, Routledge

Cohan, S. and Shires, L.M. (1988) *Telling Stories: A Theoretical Analysis of Narrative Fiction*, Routledge

Fiske, John (1989) *Understanding Popular Culture*, Unwin Hyman

Freud, Sigmund (1990) *Art and Literature*, Penguin

Friel, J. (2000) 'Reading as a Writer', in J. Newman *et al.* (eds), *The Writer's Workbook*, Arnold

Gilligan, Carol (1982) *In a Different Voice*, Harvard University Press

Goldberg, N (1991) *Wild Mind*, Bantam

Harper, G. (1997) 'Introducing Gramography', *Writing in Education*, 12

Heaney, S. (1979) *Preoccupations: Selected Prose 1968–78*, Faber & Faber

—— (1995) *The Redress of Poetry*, Faber & Faber

Hughes, T. (1968) *Poetry in the Making*, Faber & Faber

Hull, R. (2001) 'What Hope for Children's Poetry?', *Books for Keeps*, January

Hunt, Peter (1991) *Criticism, Theory, and Children's Literature*, Basil Blackwell

—— (1992) *Literature for Children, Contemporary Criticism*, Routledge

Isaacson, P. (1988) *Round Buildings, Square Buildings and Buildings that Wiggle Like a Fish*, McCrae

Johnson, Pamela (2000) 'Reading to Write: Exploring Narrative Strategies in Contemporary Short Fiction', critical study, MA in Writing, University of Glamorgan

Leeson, R. (1985) *Reading and Righting*, Collins

Lewis, C.S. (1996) *Of Other Worlds: Essays and Short Stories*, Bles

Lodge, D. (1984) *The Language of Fiction*, Routledge & Kegan Paul

—— (1990) *The Art of Fiction*, Penguin

Lubbock, P. (1926) *The Craft of Fiction*, Jonathan Cape

McKee, R. (1999) *Story*, Methuen

Middlehurst, Rob (2001) 'New Tissues of Past Citations', *Writing in Education*, 22

Mitchell, W. (ed.) (1981) *On Narrative*, University of Chicago Press

Onega, S. and Landa, J.A.G. (eds) (1996) *Narratology*, Longman Critical Readers

Peach, L. and Burton, A. (1995) *English as a Creative Art: Literary Concepts Linked to Creative Writing*, David Fulton

Pope, Rob (1995) *Textual Interventions: Critical and Creative Strategies for Literary Studies*, Routledge

Richardson, L. (1991) *Writing Strategies: Reaching Diverse Audiences*, Sage

Rosen, H. (1985) *Stories and Meanings*, Thimble Press

Saboda, C. (2000) 'White Roses at Willow Lake', MA in Writing for Children dissertation, King Alfred's, Winchester.

Sharples, Mike (1999) *How We Write*, Routledge

Sheppard, Robert (1999) 'The Poetics of Writing: The Writing of Poetics', in *Creative Writing Conference 1999, Proceedings*, Sheffield Hallam University (http://www.nawe.co.uk)

Todorov, T. (1990) *Genre in Discourse*, Cambridge University Press

Waugh, P. (1984) *Metafiction: The Theory and Practice of Self-conscious Fiction*, Methuen

Yeats, W.B. (1967) *Collected Poetry*, Macmillan

Some useful general critical writing

Adorno, Theodor (1991) *The Culture Industry*, Routledge

Auerbach, Erich (1998) *Mimesis: The Representation of Reality in Western Literature*, trans. Willard Trask, Harvard University Press

Bakhtin, Mikhail (1984) *Rabelais and his World*, Indiana University Press

Barthes, Roland (1975) *The Pleasure of the Text*, trans. Richard Miller, Hill and Wang

—— (1989) *Mythologies*, Paladin

Baudrillard, Jean (1985) 'The Ecstasy of Communication', in *Postmodern Culture*, ed. Hal Foster, Pluto Press

Benjamin, Walter (1973) *Illuminations*, trans. Harry Zohn, ed. with an introduction by Hannah Arendt, Fontana

Calvino, Italo (1986) *The Uses of Literature*, trans. Patrich Creagh, Harvest/HJB

—— (1996) *Six Memos for the Next Millennium*, Vintage

de Man, Paul (1986) *The Resistance to Theory*, Manchester University Press

Derrida, Jacques (1978) *Writing and Difference*, trans. Alan Bass, Routledge

Hall, Stuart (ed.) (1980) *Culture, Media, Language*, Hutchinson

Hardy, Thomas (1983) *Tess of the D'Urbervilles*, Penguin

Kimpton, Diana (2000) http://www.Wordpool.co.uk

Kundera, Milan (1988) *The Art of the Novel*, trans. Linda Asher, Faber & Faber.

Lacan, Jacques (1988) 'The Insistence of the Letter in the Unconscious', in David Lodge (ed.), *Modern Criticism and Theory*, Longman

Melrose, Andrew (2001) The Mouse Stone, Ginn

Melrose, Andrew and Brown, Brian (1998b) *Ready Aim Fire*, Cassell

Phillips, Adam (1995) *Terrors and Experts*, Faber & Faber

—— (2000) *Promises Promises*, Faber & Faber

Propp, Vladimir (1968) *Morphology of the Folktale*, ed. Louis Wagner and Alan Dundes, University of Texas Press

Ricour, Paul (1965) *History and Truth*, trans. Chas A. Kelbley, Northwestern University Press

Rorty, Richard (1989) *Contingency, Irony and Solidarity*, Cambridge University Press.

Stevenson, R. L. (1987) *Treasure Island*, Puffin

Warner, Marina (1994) *From the Beast to the Blonde: On Fairytales and Their Tellers*, Chatto & Windus

White, Hayden (1978) *Tropics of Discourse*, Johns Hopkins University Press

—— (1987) *The Content of the Form*, Johns Hopkins University Press

Index

A *Baby Driver Book* 89
A *Day in the Life of Ivan Denisovich*
    145
A *Kitten Called Moonlight* 99
Ahlberg, Janet and Alan 90
archaeology 21, 22
Aristotle 12, 17
Auden, W.H. 74
Austen, Jane 5
awareness 20

Balance 16
Baudrillard, J 10
Beck, Ian 100
Beginning 17–18
Beginning the beginning
    42–49
Ben the Baker 136
Benjamin, Walter 3, 10
Bettelheim, Bruno 42, 96,
    127
bible 26
Blake, Andrew 112, 114
Blake, William 145
Board books 88–89
Bob the Builder 98
Brown, Martin 151
Burgess, Melvyn, 38, 134
Butterworth, Nick 31, 101

Byatt, A.S. 8

Calvino, Italo 1, 74–75, 79
Can't You Sleep Little Bear 60–61, 93,
    98, 109
Cara a boca chiusa 106
Carle, Eric 90
Carpenter, Humphrey 136
cause and effect 17
censorship 48
Chapters 42–62
Characters 22–29
Chianti 106
cliché 7, 9, 18
clucking chickens 6
commodity fettish 10
Consequence 16–17
Copernicus 86
Cowcher, Helen 143
craft 2, 3, 11
Crafting and the critically creative
    1
craftsman 3
creative process 7
"Creative Writers and
    Daydreaming" 18
critical enquiry 12
critical perspective 3, 11
critical positioning 111

critical representation 9
critical theorists 11
criticism 12

Dahl, Roald 150
Darwin, Charles 10, 42
Deary, Terry 143–144, 151
Delillo, Don 8
Derrida, Jacques 8, 12, 21, 42
Dialogue 63–74
Dialogue tips 71–74
Dickens, Charles ix, 48, 95
Dilly the Dinosaur 36, 135–136
dinosaurs 22
Disharmony 16
Disney 11
Dorfmann, Ariel 9
Dylan, Bob 20, 42

Einstein, Albert 20, 149–150
Eliot, T.S. 3
End 17–18, 55–60
English Association 102
Erasmus 95
Essex, David 26
Evita 47
experience 9, 10

Fiction for children – a critical
    perspective 110–119
Film and new media (an
    introduction) 155
Fine, Anne 2, 35
Firth, Barbara 60, 109
Foreman, Michael 149
Four Black Puppies 102
Freud, Sigmund 10, 12, 16, 19, 129,
    149
Friel, James 8

gender difference 80
Geras, Adele 133–134
Goggle Eyes 35
Great Expectations 48

Grindley, Sally 102

Hardy, Thomas 25, 116–118
Harry Potter 7, 11, 38, 115, 118,
    131, 136
Heaney, Seamus 3
Heart of Mid-Lothian, The 143
Hissey, Jane 90
historical horizon 5
Holes 41
Hollindale, Peter 119
Hollingworth, George 101
Homo fabula 9
homo historia 21
Horowitz, Anthony 115
Horrible Histories 143
Houellebecq, Michel 42
Hull, Robert 152
Humour 150–151
Hunt, Peter 6, 91–92, 94, 118

Inciting incident 16–17
Inglis, Fred 110
Inkpen, Mick 31, 90, 101
Introduction ix – xi
Invisible Cities 79

Jasper's Beanstalk 31, 101, 103
Johnson, Samuel 115
Jolly Postman, The 90
Jung, Carl 19, 42
Junk 38, 134

Kimpton, Diana xi, 98, 108, 143,
    146–148
King Alfred's x
King Lear 69
Kipper 101
Kipper's Blue Balloon 90
Klee, Paul 7
knowledge 10

language 7
Leeson, Robert 6, 111

Letters from the Inside 38
Levi-Strauss, Claude 3
Lewis, C.S. 112–115, 118, 149
literacy   5
literary theorists 11
Lively, Penelope 2
Lodge, David 74
logos 94–95
Lolita 25
Longer fiction 84, 125–132

MA: Writing for Children xi, 2
McCurry, Ruth 6
McKee, Robert 16, 109
Madonna 46
magic formula 13
Mallett, Margaret 143
Marsden, John 38
Marx, Karl 12
Meek, Margaret 91–92, 140
Melrose, Andrew 5, 37, 103, 115,
    116, 151, 155
metaphor 7, 77–79
metonym 7
Middle 17–18, 50–55
mixed race 80
Mona Lisa x
Morecambe and Wise 3
Mouse Look Out 102
Mouse Stone, The 85, 101
Mozart, W.A. x
multicultural 80
Murphy, Jill 136

Nabokov, V. 25
Narcissus 76
Narnia 113
Nodelman, Perry 94
Non-fiction140–149
Novelty books 90
Nursery rhymes 89–90
nurture 5, 91–96

Old Bear, 90

Phillips, Adam 4, 94, 97, 152
Picture book presentation 100,
    104–108
Picture books 84, 90–109
Pictures books – a critical
    perspective 91–99
play 19
plot 17, 42–62
Poetics 12
Poetry (an introduction) 152–155
Point Horror 132
polymath 106
Pound, Ezra 3
POV (point of view) 4, 8
Powell, Anna xi
Powling, Chris 150
Previn, Andre 3
Problem 16–17
profanities 7
Prose 74–81
publishing 6, 10
Pullman, Phillip 39, 75–76, 78–79
Pyramid plot structure 13, 42–62

Rachmaninov 2
Rasselas 115
Read aloud books 121–122
Reading abilities 84–86
real time 99
red herring 55
Rees, Celia 131–132
representation 9
Resolution 16–17
Rose, Jacqueline 4, 97, 128–129
Rowling, J.K 7, 38, 136
'rule of three' 103
Rushdie, Salman 2

Saboda, Carol 40–41
Sachar, Louis 41
Sainsbury, Lisa 155
St Jerome 94
San Gimignano 106
Scott, Walter 143

Scrutton, Clive 102
secret 13
Sendak, Maurice 96
Sensory books 84
serendipity 7
Series Fiction 135–137
Shakespeare, William ix
Shooting Joe 20, 21, 23–26, 39–40, 47–62
Short fiction, 84, 109–125
simile 77–79
Snow not tell 28–29
Solzhenitsyn, Alexander 145
Some useful critical books on children's literature and storytelling 159
Some useful general critical writing 162–163
Some useful works on critical and creative writing 160–162
Sophocles 21
Squirtle 106
Stevenson, Robert Louise 127
Stormbreaker 115
Story 15–22
story 3, 11
Story bridge 102
Storykeepers, The 145–146
storyteller 16
storytelling 3
Subplot 42–62

Teen fiction 84, 132–139
telling stories 3
Tess of the D'Urbevilles 25, 116–118
The Aha! 56–60
Thomas the Tank Engine 98

Tony Bradman 36
Treasure Island 111, 118
Tucker, Nicholas 87, 91–92, 113, 115, 133, 137

Unheimlich 12, 128
unwritten rules 6, 7

Very Hungry Caterpillar, The 90
viewpoint 7
Viewpoint: Objective 30–32; Subjective 32–41; Omniscient 32–34; First person 34–36; Second Person 30; Third person 36–41; Third person unlimited 36–38; Third person limited 38–41; Virtual first person 40–41

Waddell, Martin 60, 109
Waite, Judy 102, 135
War Boy 149
Watson, Victor 135
White, Hayden 145
Wilson, Jacqueline 39
Winchester Cathedral x
Wind in the Willows, The 111
Winnie the Pooh 11
word waltzing 80
Worst Witch 136
Write the height 83–139
Write the rest 140–158
Write the rights 15–81
www.wordpool.co.uk xi, 146

Zipes, Jack 11, 97, 115, 116, 137